Second Edition

TEACHING ETHNIC AND GENDER AWARENESS

Methods and Materials for the Elementary School

EDITH W. KING
University of Denver

KENDALL/HUNT PUBLISHING COMPANY
2460 Kerper Boulevard P.O. Box 539 Dubuque, Iowa 52004-0539

Formerly entitled *Teaching Ethnic Awareness*

Copyright © 1980 by Goodyear Publishing Company, Inc.

Copyright © 1990 by Kendall/Hunt Publishing Company

Library of Congress Catalog Card Number: 89–62837

ISBN 0–8403–5610–2

Printed in the United States of America
10 9 8 7 6 5 4 3 2 1

Contents

PART I
What Has Race, Class and Gender in Education to Do
with Elementary School Teachers?

Chapter 1
What Is Ethnicity? Why Is It Important in the Elementary School Program?, 3

Chapter 2
Pluralism in Education, 19

Chapter 3
The Impact of Race, Class and Gender on Diversity in Education, 33

Chapter 4
Dealing with Difference in School, Community, and Nation, 45

Chapter 5
The Teacher of Young Children as Researcher in Multicultural Settings, 69

Chapter 6
Future Directions for Teaching Ethnic and Gender Awareness, 83

PART II
Activities for Recognizing Ethnicity, Social Class and Gender in the Elementary School

For my daughter, Melissa, and my son, Matthew
. . . and their search for a life in a non-sexist,
multicultural, global society.

Preface

In the decade that has passed since the first edition of this book, events and trends have reshaped and extended multicultural and multiethnic education. Now awareness of diversity includes gender and social class differences. Exceptionality in other dimensions such as handicappism, giftedness and even ageism influences the conditions of teaching in our classrooms as we approach the 21st Century.

The second edition of *Teaching Ethnic and Gender Awareness: Methods and Materials for the Elementary School* is designed in two major parts. Part I brings into focus the rationale for sensitivity and awareness of the status of diversity and pluralism in American culture. This new edition urges teachers to recognize that race, class and gender differences can no longer be ignored in our elementary school classrooms. Chapter One introduces the themes that now enlarge the concept of multicultural education to include sexism, classism and discrimination on the basis of cultural differences. Definitions of key terms and concepts are provided for the reader, as well.

Chapters Two and Three discuss the effects of pluralism in education in today's worldwide society and what this means for the teacher, personally, as well as for the students in the classroom. Chapter Four looks at how to utilize multiculturalism in the classroom and in the community to enrich and enhance our teaching. A unique and exemplary early elementary school is featured in this chapter. Chapter Five presents ways for and examples of how teachers of young children can take up the role of researcher in the multicultural settings of the school, neighborhood and community. Chapter Six explores future directions for ethnic awareness and multicultural education, urging a combination of multicultural education, global education strategies and gender awareness as the desired educational format in our contemporary worldwide society.

Part II presents activities for classrooms that recognize the ethnic, social class and gender diversity that exist in the elementary school. These activities are practical, with teacher tested exercises that really work in the curriculum for children ages four to twelve years. Finally, an annotated bibliography for the teacher encourages further investigation and readings on race, class and gender awareness in our schools and classrooms.

Acknowledgments

The second edition of this book has come to fruition because of the enthusiasm and encouragement of my associates, my students, undergraduate and graduate, my friends and my family. Many teachers contributed to the development of the first and now the second edition. However, the impetus and excitement of working with the teachers, the students and the principal of University Park Early Elementary School, Denver, Colorado and their contributions to this volume is what, I feel, has made this a unique book in multicultural education. I want to extend my thanks in particular to: Dr. Karen Harvey, Principal, Gloria Doğan, ESL Teacher, Janet Zander and Wendy Cameron, Kindergarten Teachers, Joanne Greenberg, Gifted and Talented Teacher, and Susan West, Artist-in-Residence of the University Park School.

Another colleague and collaborator in early childhood education research and classroom teaching methods, Dr. Marjorie Milan, provided much support and insight for the book. And my thanks are due to teacher-educators: Dr. Sharon LaPierre, Roselie Bambrey and Dr. Margery Camaren; and to wordprocessor, Kimberly Mills, and my editor, Jon Baillie.

What Has Race, Class and Gender in Education to Do with Elementary School Teachers?

What is Ethnicity? Why Is It Important in the Elementary School Program?

The Era of Ethnic Literacy

A child asks her parents, "What are our roots? What is my heritage?" Current projects and programs in our classrooms plus the continual emphasis on television of traditions, heritage, and "roots" have heightened young children's awareness of ethnic identification, ethnic differences and the labels people use for their nationality, heritage or membership in a sociocultural group.

Ethnicity affects almost everyone. It affects our behavior in the social spheres of our lives, may affect how we spend our money, how we vote, even where we live or where we go out to dine. Privately we use ethnicity as a filter for forming our identities, opinions and attitudes toward others. Individuals function on a continuum of ethnic affiliation ranging from nonrecognition of one's ethnicity in daily life to an almost complete identification with an ethnic group in all activities, choices, and designations of self-identification.

Because ethnic affiliation is central to many people's images and concepts of self-identity, teachers need to be aware of the importance of multiculturalism in expanding the elementary school child's opportunities to learn. That is, requirements or cultural conditioning inherent in the ethnic group a child identifies with may influence his or her learning options.

Throughout this book we will provide many examples and anecdotes detailing the affects of cultural conditioning and ethnic affiliation on young children. Just to raise the issue let us recognize that a child may be a member of a racial or ethnic minority group, what is currently termed a visible minority group (Black, Chicano, Native American or Asian American), and this affiliation may be a stigma as well as a handicap for the young learner. Or a child may be a member of an ethnic group that does not display an obvious physical difference from the White Anglo majority society (Polish American, Italian American, Jewish American). This affiliation could deeply influence the quality of the child's learning experiences although the teacher may be totally unaware that such a situation exists. This type of ethnic group membership may be reinforced by geographic location, such as residence in the urban ghettos of Boston, Philadelphia or New York.

Ethnic affiliation has implications for the teacher's awareness and sensitivities, as well as for the student's group memberships. If we are calling for an awareness of ethnic identification and heritage in education, we must provide techniques for acquiring such sensitivities and knowledge. This is the process that ethnic educators have labeled "ethnic literacy" (Banks, 1975, 1987). Ethnic literacy has been defined as a knowledge of the role and function ethnicity has in our daily lives, in our society, and in our transactions, locally, regionally and transnationally. Ethnic or crosscultural literacy also encompasses understandings of intergroup relations and ethnic conflict. Ethnic educators have even devised pencil and paper tests for teachers to assess their status on ethnic literacy and competence (Banks, 1986, pp. 125–127).

Developing ethnic literacy with children and their teachers calls upon us to acquaint the school with the traditions of the home and family. This lack of recognition of the culture and heritage a child brings to school is a stumbling block that could be one of the most serious educational deficiencies facing us today; one that ethnic education attempts to overcome. It is time that the elementary school take the initiative and develop linkages between ethnicity and education. It is with this challenge in mind that this resource book is prepared for those teachers concerned with the inadequacies in the present school curriculum and how to correct them.

Differentiating Multiethnic Education from Teaching about Minorities

Recently many teachers have made concerted efforts to include activities that involve the study of minority groups in their programs sometime during the school year. Materials have now been developed at all grade levels to teach about Black, Hispanic or Native Americans, contributions to our society. This curriculum material is usually placed in social studies, and occasionally with language arts or reading activities.

Since the 1970s, some reading materials and social studies textbooks have been revised to include references to and pictures of Blacks, Native Americans, Asian Americans and Hispanics. Media material such as filmstrips, films and videos, photos and posters include information on these same ethnic groups. But this is not multicultural education nor the consideration of ethnicity in the curriculum. Rather, it is recognition of the contributions to American life of some other groups of people than the "majority" white, Anglo Saxon Protestants who have traditionally been assumed to represent the culture and heritage of our country.

What, then, is multiethnic education and a regard for multiculturalism? It is the recognition, and hence, the inclusion of the heritage, history, traditions, and customs, language or linguistic style, other contributions and the on-going lifestyle of the many cultures and ethnic groups that constitute American society. In our schools, especially at the elementary level, we need to provide more than the dominant or majority perspective. This means that, in the teaching of reading and language arts, history, geography, social studies, math, science, music and art, elementary school teachers should be conscious and aware of multiethnic approaches. These multiethnic approaches include the processes of perception of human differences and commonalities and how they influence the way we deal with people.

Too often, minority studies at the elementary school level have taken on superficial and spurious forms when including materials about the many ethnic groups in American life— "THE Italians"; "THE Greeks"; "THE Irish"; "THE Arabs" and so on. A common pitfall in this context is the listing of heroes or well-known personalities of the ethnic or minority group. This gives children a romanticized and distorted view of the ethnic group and encourages stereotyping. Those people are all good athletes or outstanding musicians—or whatever the model or hero chosen. Hero worship usually only highlights the contributions of the well-known men (rarely women) of the ethnic group, since our society historically has left out the work and contributions of women of all ethnic or minority groups, as well as women of the dominant group.

What is really needed in the inclusion of ethnic customs and rituals is understanding what lies behind the overt acts and expressions. What does the dance, the artwork or the special food mean in the context of the culture and tradition, the heritage and the daily life of the group from which it comes? And how does this custom compare and contrast to what is commonly expected in American life?

Thus, we no longer see the school in America as an agency for implementing the "melting pot" doctrine or the idea that we are all Americans and can be melted down into one homogeneous group of people. With the importance that diversity now plays in American life, our political and social leaders are calling for cultural pluralism—diverse cultures and subgroups living together with mutual respect and understanding. Although there are other approaches, cultural pluralism provides a more accurate lens for looking at school life. Ethnic education in the classroom should help to develop an acceptance, appreciation and empathy for the rich cultural and linguistic diversity in America.

The Aspects of Ethnicity

To begin teaching about ethnicity teachers must be equipped with a sense of their own ethnic and personal identity, self awareness and positive acceptance of their group affiliation. Unique likes and dislikes must be recognized by the teacher before ethnic education can occur in the classroom. This means that the teacher must be aware of how he or she was socialized as a child and young adult, what values and customs were internalized and continue to be followed as the result of personal and group affiliations. Teachers need to accept and feel comfortable with their ethnicity and then respond positively to individuals who belong to other ethnic groups. This is a lifelong process.

We are rapidly moving toward an American group life characterized by cultural diversity and the widespread support of cultural pluralism in every sector of our society—social, economic, political, religious and educational spheres. Many educators have rejected the idea of assimilation: that immigrants and foreigners permanently living in the United States should absorb the "American Way of Life" recognizing that there is more than one way to be an American. The America First or American Way perspective, have been eschewed in many school districts for policies stressing that Americans can live in a global society and a world context.

Americans become acculturated as they pass from generation to generation, leaving their immigrant experience behind. Acculturation influences people to change and reshape customs and patterns of behavior to incorporate new and different folkways. Interesting and colorful customs blending traditions and cultures are created through the process of acculturation and cultural diffusion.

Acculturation is occurring in America today. It leads us toward a culturally pluralistic society, a society that values the traditions and practices that are uniquely Polish American, Italian American, Jewish American, Mexican American, etc. American ethnic groups with ties to nations around the globe are still uniquely American, though they originated far from the United States. The process of acculturation, the subtle changing of ways and traditions, is also experienced by ethnic groups with origins in the United States—our American Indians.

In our cities and towns in this past decade new waves of immigrants from the far corners of the globe, from lands and cultures little known to Americans, have come to take up permanent residence. These new waves of immigrant families from Vietnam, Laos and other areas of the Far East, Middle East, from Central America and even the African continent are fleeing their native countries due to political and social upheavals. Suddenly many American elementary schools are filled with children speaking no English, but rather speaking the languages of the many new immigrant groups—Farsi, Urdu, Hindi, Arabic, Vietnamese, Lao, Hmong, Khmer, Korean and other languages unfamiliar to teachers and administrators. These conditions of wide diversity of school populations have been experienced in other developed nations.

We cannot expect teachers and administrators in our schools to learn to speak all the languages of the children they now are dealing with or will come to deal with. But we can give teachers crosscultural techniques and strategies to use in their teaching of children with widely differing ethnic and cultural heritages. Helping teachers to view the world from the others' vantage points will greatly enhance their effectiveness with ALL children. In the teaching of the social studies (history, geography, civics and economics) as well as the arts and humanities, it is essential that teachers be sensitive and aware of the differing interpretations that children from diverse cultures hold. Further, these "differences" which are often regarded as a problem, can be turned into a resource as teachers learn to integrate the ethnic heritages represented in the classroom into a platform for studying varying cultural perspectives within pluralistic traditions.

To better understand the specific conditions, attitudes, climates and dynamics in an ethnicaly diverse elementary school classroom, we offer the following account.

A Muslim Child in an American School

The children of Aspen pod, the ten to eleven year olds at Ponderosa Elementary School, were back in their open space classroom after the visit to Center City Art museum. The group of children, ninety or so, and their teaching staff of seven adults were still milling around the multipurpose area talking about the experiences of the day's outing. But the most discussed event was Ahmed's behavior at the museum. Ahmed had come to the school just this September when his parents moved to the United States from Beirut. All the children in Aspen pod knew Ahmed was very different. He was Muslim, dark-skinned, "very smart" everyone said, and excellent in math. His behavior at the museum today had astonished everyone—children and teachers alike.

Our scene shifts to earlier that day. We are in the museum scanning the featured exhibit— "Costumery, Clothing and Jewelry of the World's Peoples." Now we see Ahmed, standing as though transfixed before a large glass display case filled with robes and headdresses and several pieces of jewelry. His eyes are fixed on a stunning sliver necklace. With his face pressed to the glass of the case he seems oblivious of the children calling to him, urging him. "Ahmed, it's time to go! The bus is here! Mrs. James is coming now! We HAVE to leave!"

Some of the children come up behind Ahmed. Aaron, his closest associate since he joined Aspen pod, tugs at his shirt sleeve, indicating his concern. Ahmed does not move, his eyes seem riveted to the shining object in the glass case. Finally Mrs. James, the head teacher of the group, arrives on the scene. She observes Ahmed for a few moments then bends down to speak to him. "What is it Ahmed? What is there in the case that is so important to you?" she whispers softly to the boy.

"See that KIRDALA, the KIRDALA!" is Ahmed's response, his voice trembling with excitement. "It is just like ours: just like my mother's! It was given to us—from our cousins, the Badaawi!"

The teacher is puzzled. A KIRDALA, what is that? Mrs. James quickly scans the descriptions of the items listed at the foot of the display case. Yes! there it is! Item Number 6.

"Bedouin choker necklace, or KIRDALA, from Northeast Arabia. This fine example displays several characteristics of Bedouin (Badaawi) jewelry; pendant bells, red and blue stones, filigree and simple hook clasp. This necklace illustrates the ancient style and elegance that has become apparent in Bedouin jewelry since the Egyptian influence and the opening of Tutankhaamun's tomb in 1922." This quote is from *Bedouin Jewelry in Saudi Arabia* by Heather C. Ross London: Stacey International, 1978, p. 31.

The commotion continues around Ahmed: children shouting. Now more adults' voices joining in urging that it is time to leave. Mrs. James thinks quickly. "Yes, Ahmed, that is a beautiful KIRDALA. We must go now but perhaps you can have your mother bring yours, the KIRDALA of your family to show us at school. I know we would all like to see such a beautiful necklace again." Ahmed turns to the teacher; it is the first time since he initially noticed the beautiful Bedouin necklace that he takes his eyes off the object. "Could I really show everyone? Do you think Mother would bring it to show everyone? It is a great treasure in our family. We are proud of this KIRDALA. It has much history as you here say."

"I'd sure like to see it," Aaron speaks up now, still tugging at Ahmed's sleeve. The small group of children remaining with Mrs. James take their leave of the exhibit room, as Ahmed's eyes return searching for one last glimpse of the treasured necklace.

Relating Learning Experiences to Aspects of Ethnicity

With this account we launch into an introduction that will discuss the details of relating learning experiences to ethnically diverse populations. First it is appropriate to state that we believe that all children need to be aware of and sensitized to the multicultural nature of their society, whether there are members of diverse ethnic groups in their classroom or not. With this in mind let us examine major concepts in ethnic and multicultural education. These major aspects of ethnicity are:

- the *historical* aspects of cultures and heritages
- the *geographic* aspects of cultures, nationalities and ethnic enclaves
- the *linguistic* variations between peoples and across language groups
- the *religious* aspects that include the customs, ceremonies and traditions associated with different belief systems
- the *social class* aspects and their economic implications
- the *political* aspects including international or transnational ties
- the *moral* aspects or stereotyping, prejudice and racism—the negative aspects of ethnicity

Now let us turn to a discussion of each of the aspects of ethnicity. The HISTORICAL component of ethnicity and multicultural education is the most obvious aspect. It comes immediately into recognition as we examine the phenomenon of ethnicity. It is the sharing of a heritage, often ancient and revered, that brings people together in an ethnic group identification. For example, museums and historical societies everywhere, as described in the account of Ahmed and the kirdala, are filled with exhibits of artifacts and relics of many peoples who comprise the nationality and ethnic groups of the society. When discussing and considering the attributes of an ethnic group one must take up its historical development, whether in the recent past or going back generations and even centuries to recount the origin of its traditions, myths and legends. An historical perspective of an ethnic group increases understanding of the particular group of people, their art, music, drama, and literature.

Allied to the historical is the GEOGRAPHIC aspect of ethnicity, an essential component in the formation of ethnic groups. We are continually aware of how people left their native homelands in the "Old World" to journey to the new land and found colonies and settlements in geographic locations similiar to their native lands. Literature often includes large and carefully detailed maps of migration patterns, initial settlements and areas of habitation and population. These maps and displays clearly indicate to the readers WHY people moved, as well as where they settled in various locations, how natural forces influenced the settlements, and where the mingling of ethnic groups occurred. Feature articles including large, foldout maps, beautifully illustrated, in the *National Geographic Magazine* published in the United States and widely distributed are excellent examples of how geography can be utilized to understand better the ethnic background of a people.

Language is inherent in the ability to communicate and is critical to group identity and affiliation. The LINGUISTIC aspect of ethnicity is an essential component with which all teachers must deal. Socio-linguist Joshua Fishman states this eloquently when he writes that ethnicity is one of the inevitable attributes of social life. He reminds us that new ethnicities arise, old ones alter, and others disappear, but people cannot exist without their language that is deeply tied to their ethnicity. (Fishman, 1976). Language is the medium through which the individual makes sense of the everyday world. Therefore, one's language is intricately entwined in self-identity and self-concept. If teachers do not accept a student's language, they are certainly rejecting that student.

Religion, too, plays a central role in the life of ethnic groups. Religious ceremonies, rituals and festivals often entail using elaborate artifacts, sacred objects, icons, and special items. Religious ceremonies are carried out in magnificent buildings like the great cathedrals of Europe, or in more humble settings like rural churches and mosques. But the impact of religion on ethnicity cannot be understated. For some ethnic groups religious identity and observances fill every waking hour and almost every mundane act. Religious practice is not, nor ever has been, limited to national boundaries or secular states.

Intimately tied to geographical and religious aspects of ethnicity are the SOCIAL CLASS and economic affiliations of groups. One cannot examine the lives of people without touching on the social class structure of the group or subgroup. Economic wherewithal is tied to accumulation of material goods and the amassing of treasured arts as wealth. What is treasured and valued comes from the worth imbued to the material good, such as precious metals and jewels, through a cultural definition of what is valuable. Further, accumulation

of wealth and status means power and superiority over other groups. Social and economic status tends to give one group power over another and leads to attitudes that one ethnic or racial group is inherently better than another because it is richer and holds a higher social status.

Material wealth not only endows an individual or group with greater social status, often it is accompanied by wider political power. POLITICAL aspects are reflected in ethnic group affiliation. Electing officials to public office or influencing the passage of particular laws can be effected by ethnic power blocs. Treaties and agreements between nations, also, can be influenced by ethnic affiliations, alliances or antipathies—all political aspects of ethnicity.

This recognition of the political and economic component leads to the negative aspects of ethnicity and multiculturalism—the stereotyping, prejudice and racism that are labeled the MORAL aspects of ethnicity. These, too, are part of human nature. Racism can be formal, institutionalized, written into the laws of the land; or racism can be informal, personal subtle acts of exclusion and rejection. These negative aspects of ethnicity are part of history and often are evident in our attitudes and in our customs. Accounts of discrimination and prejudice can be obvious and blatant, such as the treatment of Native Americans in the United States during the nineteenth and twentieth centuries when their lands and settlements were summarily appropriated. Sometimes discrimination is evidenced more indirectly, as in the inability of ethnic minority artists to have their work accepted and valued by the majority culture.

To summarize: the historical, geographic, religious, social class, economic, political and linguistic aspects of ethnicity intertwine in dynamic relationships to define an individual's or group's heritage, roots, and identity. To teach effectively for a multicultural society, it is important to recognize the complexity of the concept of ethnicity.

Racism, Sexism and Classism in the United States

It was noted that the aspects of ethnicity present positive, creative and enabling views of ethnicity. Only the moral aspects, descriptions of racism, prejudice and discrimination point to the negative, deleterious aspects of ethnic identification. Discrimination and prejudice come in many forms. In recent years social scientists have moved to differentiate and delineate the various forms of discrimination, labeling them as sexism and classism, as well as racism. Other forms of discrimination are termed ageism and handicappism or exceptionality. For the purposes of this volume we will focus on racism, sexism and classism. Now let us examine briefly each of these "isms."

RACISM: It has been difficult for social scientists to clearly define racism. Sociologist Peter Rose notes that racism refers to a special kind of prejudice, a prejudice directed against those who are thought to possess biologically or socially inherited characteristics that set them apart. Institutionalized racism is characterized by ingrained prejudices reflected in customs and laws concerning what is expected, what is required, what is forbidden to the marked groups or individuals. (Rose, 1974)

The importance of physical characteristics in the dynamics of prejudice and racism has been elaborated on by most authorities on the subject. Whiteness and white supremacy have been the central focus in discussions of what influences racism in the United States. Although skin color appears as one of the most frequent stimuli for racist behavior, both historically and geographically, differing examples from other societies can be drawn.

For instance, Puerto Rican children migrating from Puerto Rico to mainland America have experienced problems related to skin color that were unknown to them in Puerto Rico, where Whites and Blacks mix freely and intermarry more frequently than in the U.S. Skin color in Puerto Rico is less important in determining class level. Although Whites are more likely to be in the upper classes, social relationships are more important in determining membership in the upper classes.

Yet in the United States, Puerto Ricans and other ethnic groups such as East Indians and Middle Easterners, who are of intermediate skin color, experience difficulties and problems due to their pigmentation. Often these groups of people are alienated from both Blacks and Whites in U.S. communities.

The dynamics of racism were brilliantly presented in Gordon Allport's classic book *The Nature of Prejudice,* where he wrote, "Race is a fashionable focus for the propaganda of alarmists and demagogues. It is the favorite bogey used by those who themselves are suffering from some nameless dread. Racists seem to be people who, out of their own anxieties, have manufactured the demon of race." (Allport, 1954, p. 108) These statements characterize the personal or informal aspects of racism, the psychological needs of individuals that cause them to stereotype, scapegoat and discriminate. Both forms of racism, institutional and informal, are used against the stigmatized group to provide a rationale for why they cannot or should not succeed in our society.

SEXISM: Sexism has been identified as attitudes and practices that discriminate against an individual solely on the basis of being female. Sexism is the unintended and unwitting granting of power and privilege to men over women. Based in tradition and a result of unexamined actions and practices, sex discrimination is revealed in daily family life, in the world of work, in schools and classrooms, in the books and magazines we read, in the media, in political and international relations.

Historically, women have experienced discrimination in hiring and promotion. When we focus on the schools and education, studies have shown that the only reasons given for not hiring or promoting women have only to do with the fact that they were female. Tradition-bound statements such as "women are not hired for this position because none has ever held this job before; or, men do not want to take directions from a woman; or, the community is not ready for a woman principal,"—all reasons that have to do with the individual's sex and not ability, training or competence. Further, school districts advertise that they would hire women and minority teachers and administrators, but that no qualified applicants apply, while discounting these very applications. (Shakeshaft, 1987, p. 96–7).

Sexism in schools is manifested in the curriculum materials found in every classroom. Specific forms of gender bias have been identified by Sadker and Sadker in their extensive work on sex equity. These forms of gender bias include:

- linguistic or language usage—use of masculine terms and pronouns exclusively, most prevalent among these terms being "man" and "mankind";
- stereotyping boys' versus girls' roles, attitudes, values, and behaviors;
- omitting women's contributions or keeping them invisible by systematically excluding any mention of information referring to girls and women;
- presenting only one interpretation of an issue, situation, or group; thereby creating an imbalance which acknowledges only the male perspective;
- portraying unrealistically American life, with the controversy and conflict removed so that young readers are led to believe there really are no single parents or troubled families;
- fragmenting the contributions of women as unique occurrences, or separating information about women (and minorities) into special sections that indicate these are exceptional cases. (Sadker and Sadker, 1982) The literature on the subject of sexism has proliferated in recent years as a new awareness of this form of discrimination has swelled.

CLASSISM: This manifestation of discrimination arises from the wide inequities in the distribution of wealth in our nation, which have grown even greater in recent years. Sociologists depict American society as consisting of three major socio-economic classes—upper, middle and lower. Lately the inequities in the distribution of wealth have been so disparate that the number of those considered to be middle class have been shrinking while the lower classes have grown twice as rapidly as the upper class. (Sleeter and Grant, 1988) This situation points to a widening gap between the rich and the poor in our country.

Classism's impact on education and schools is stated in reports of inequalities in educational opportunities. Caroline Persell, who has written and researched extensively this area of educational inequalities, notes that the profile of social class differences in education in the United States has been oversimplified. She points out that social class backgrounds affect where students go to school and what happens to them once they are there. Achievement testing and tracking based on these group administered tests result in lower class students' placement in programs that bring about the "self-fulfilling prophesy" of failure and school dropout. (Persell, 1977 & 1989)

In this section we have discussed three types of discrimination and prejudicial treatment toward individuals—racism, sexism and classism. At this point in our book it is useful to provide the reader some definitions of key terms in the field of ethnic education and multiculturalism.

Definitions of Key Terms

The information about ethnicity and the teaching of multicultural education presented in this book raises some specialized terms and concepts. They include words like assimilation, socialization, enculturation, acculturation, cultural pluralism, cultural diversity, the "melting pot" theory and ethnocentrism. The following reference list contains key terms and definitions frequently used in this book.

- **Ethnicity.** A sense of peoplehood and commonality derived from kinship patterns, a shared historical past, common experiences, religious affiliations, language or linguistic commonalities, shared values, attitudes, perceptions, modes of expression and identity.
- **Ethnic Identity.** The personal dimension of ethnicity or how one identifies oneself. A person is an ethnic if he or she chooses to be called an ethnic.
- **Ethnic Group.** A group of people, within a larger society, which has a common ancestry and history.
- **Ethnic Minority Group.** An ethnic or racial group that has unique physical characteristics which make its members easily identifiable and, hence, often victims of discrimination.
- **Cultural pluralism.** The process by which a variety of ethnic cultures have been able to share in the common expression of American culture and ideals.
- **Cultural Diversity.** The condition of wide diversity and differences within and among ethnic groups. Such factors as social class, occupation and lifestyles affect cultural diversity.
- **Socialization (Enculturation).** The dynamic process of internalizing the values of one's group of people. Socialization is a lifelong process.
- **Assimilation.** Sometimes called the "melting pot" theory, the absorption of a group of people or a person into the major group of the society. The giving up of unique and particular ways and mores to practice the ways and traditions of the majority.
- **Acculturation.** The subtle process of taking on new cultural traits and folkways when interacting with new and different groups of people.
- **Ethnocentrism.** The attitude that one's traditions, customs, language and values are the only way of doing things and that all others' ways (including language) are inadequate or wrong.
- **Racism.** Action often backed by theories which justify the oppression of socially stigmatized groups and attribute their status to inherited inferior traits rather than lack of opportunities and economic mobility in the society.
- **Sexism.** Discriminatory attitudes and actions towards individuals solely because they are female.
- **Classism.** Discriminatory attitudes and actions towards individuals based upon their social class affiliation.

These definitions are for the teacher's use and knowledge. Upper elementary school children, ages nine to twelve, will probably be able to use and comprehend the concepts of: ethnic group; ethnic identity; what it means to be in a minority group; being prejudiced or experiencing prejudice. These children will also understand what it means to have diversity—differences that are equally valid, and the idea that everyone does not have to be doing or following exactly the same practices and customs in a group of people.

Younger elementary school children, ages eight to ten, will mention related ideas or words like "ancestors," "customs," "immigrant," and "prejudice" when a discussion about ethnic groups is undertaken. The teacher should explain, elaborate on and interpret the terms we have listed above, rather than assuming that these ideas are too complex or beyond young children's understanding. Experience with the teaching of ethnic heritage studies in elementary school classrooms reinforces my opinion that young children can comprehend and understand what ethnicity means, especially when it is part of their daily lives.

With young children, ages four to seven, in the early childhood setting, concrete examples, illustrations and direct experience can be emphasized when discussing ethnicity. Teachers of young children should be encouraged to try discussion and experiences including field trips involving ethnic education. Sadly, too often early childhood teachers feel that such subjects are far beyond the comprehension of four to six year olds, and they dismiss the possibilities for any type of experiences or activities on a topic like ethnic education, racism, or sexism. In this book, activities in ethnic education are presented for four-to-five-year olds, as well as for children in the total range of the elementary school years.

Tips for Teaching to Reduce Discrimination

There is no doubt that teachers are powerful influences in the lives of the young children they teach. But teachers, in turn, work within a school climate and within the bureaucratic organization of a school district. Teachers should recognize that they cannot stand alone to press for pluralistic components in their classroom curriculum without commitments to ethnic education at the school and district level.

A number of studies in educational administration reveal the importance of the building principal in setting the style, climate and social atmosphere of the school, all working to develop an "esprit de corps" among members of the school faculty. Classroom teachers are affected by other school district administrators, as well. Although there is a degree of professional autonomy enjoyed by elementary school classroom teachers, it is generally agreed that they come under the constant pressure of the rules, directions and evaluations from administrative layers above. Most teachers recognize this situation consciously or unconsciously and modify their teaching styles accordingly. But a teacher's personal commitment to multiethnic education, to pluralistic and cross-cultural teaching can create new and unique situations which the teacher should be alerted to and ready to deal with. The teacher advocating multiethnic education and eschewing racism, sexism and classism in the educational setting must cultivate a school-wide and district-wide recognition of the importance of such a stance.

16

Multiethnic and pluralistic education should not be regarded as compensatory education for children who are "different" and need to be taught about the American way of life. Leading multicultural educators (Banks and Banks, 1989; Sleeter and Grant, 1988; Gollnick and Chinn, 1986; Lynch, 1987) set forth strategies for the advancement of cultural pluralism, non-sexist education, and multicultural education. They note that school district leadership, as well as parents and the broader community, must validate the need for multicultural and non-sexist education; schooling that recognizes the impact of race, class and gender upon learning. School administrators must accept the challenge to provide for comprehensive planning to incorporate these aspects in all areas of the curriculum.

Part II of this book contains field-tested activities for the elementary school classroom which implement the philosophy on multicultural education discussed here. In the activity "A Checklist on Ethnic and Non-Sexist Education for your School," we encourage teachers to ascertain the climate of the school, the school district and community. Discuss the planned experience with your principal. Be sure you have the support of significant leaders in your school before undertaking an assessment of the climate of pluralistic, non-sexist education. All this preparation will give the teacher an indication of the degree of commitment to these educational principles in the school building and in the school district.

References

Allport, Gordon. *The Nature of Prejudice.* Garden City, N.J.: Doubleday Anchor Books, 1954.

Banks, James A. *Teaching Strategies for Ethnic Studies.* Boston: Allyn and Bacon, 1975; 1979; 1984; 1987.

————. *Multiethnic Education: Theory and Practice.* Boston: Allyn and Bacon, 1981; 1988.

Banks, James A. and Banks, Cherry. (editors) *Multicultural Education; Issues and Perspectives.* Boston: Allyn and Bacon. 1989.

Barth, Frederick. *Ethnic Groups and Boundaries.* Boston: Little, Brown and Co. 1969.

Fishman, Joshua. *Bilingual Education; An International Sociological Perspective.* Rowley, Mass. Newbury House Publishers, 1976.

Gollnick, Donna and Chinn, Philip. *Multicultural Education in a Pluralistic Society.* Columbus: Merrill Publishing Co. 1986.

Glazer, Nathan and Moynihan, Daniel P. *Ethnicity; Theory and Experience.* M.I.T. Press, 1975.

Lynch, James. *Prejudice Reduction and the Schools.* New York: Nichols Publishing Co. 1987.

Multicultural Leader. Quarterly Newsletter published by the Educational Materials and Service Center, 144 Railroad Avenue, Edmonds, Wash. 98020.

Persell, Caroline H. *Education and Inequality.* New York: The Free Press. 1977.

Rose, Peter. I. *They and We; Racial and Ethnic Relations in The United States.* New York: Random House, 1974.

Ross, Heather. *Bedouin Jewelry in Saudi Arabia.* London: Stacey International, 1978.

Sadker, Myra and Sadker, David. *Sex Equity Handbook for Schools.* New York: Longman, 1982.

Shakeshaft, Carol. *Women in Educational Administration.* Newbury Park. Sage Publishing Co. 1987.

Sleeter, Christine and Grant, Carl. *Making Choices for Multicultural Education; Five Approaches to Race, Class and Gender.* Columbus, Ohio, 1988.

2

Pluralism in Education

There is always the fear that by encouraging differences among students, we might be encouraging hostility and conflict among them as well. The ethnic, racial and gender conflicts of the 1980's that have succeeded the clashes of the 1970's seem to be tearing our society apart. No educator wants to widen the polarization, but change always carries its risks as well as its possible reward, and we must attempt to improve relations among groups in whatever way we can. It would be facile to think that curriculum innovations alone could solve such a complex problem as group conflict. But a school curriculum which embraced pluralistic education might contribute to the amelioration of these conflicts while preparing children to become citizens of a multicultural society and a multiethnic world.

Pluralistic education means responding to and enhancing the culture that each child brings into the classroom. While some maintain that certain children bring no culture with them, in fact, everybody has a culture. The question is, how do the school and the teacher greet the culture, heritage and tradition that each child brings to the school when he or she enters it?

Our American Heritage in a Shrinking World

In a certain sense, all of us living in the United States are socialized by the majority society. We are "Americans All." Our Anglo Saxon majority culture is the cement which holds the country together. Our political system and our social ideals have been profoundly influenced by seventeenth and eighteenth century Englishmen. The cultural pluralism we seek will exist within the context of a strong belief in the viability of the Constitution and the ideals of a democratic republic.

We all share a heritage of distinctly American traditions, occasions such as the Fourth of July, Labor Day and Memorial Day, and most recently Martin Luther King's Birthday (that has become controversial in some states), which we commemorate with parades, gatherings and picnics. Our public schools have been the social institution for inculcating the customs, traditions and folklore of the majority (Anglo) American heritage. It is a proud tradition and one we do not wish to banish or relinquish.

Our museums and historical societies from coast to coast, in great cities and in small towns, exhibit relics and artifacts that represent this heritage which, after 200 years of existence, has evolved into a uniquely American ethnicity. This Americanism, a beautiful heritage, should not be cast aside in the endeavor to grant recognition and power to diverse ethnic groups. What we are calling for is ETHNIC PLURALISM, the opportunity for our many subcultures and ethnic groups to participate in American group life and to enrich American traditions with myriad variations of expressions, customs and folkways that make life interesting and stimulating.

The Impact of Pluralism in Education

Following are three underlying assumptions for pluralistic education. We will list them first, then elaborate on their meanings and implications for teaching.

1. Knowing one's own identity, knowing who you really are; one's heritage and traditions. Who are YOUR people? What are their practices, customs and ways?

2. Knowing about other groups in the nation. What groups other than your own are present in American society? What are their traditions, customs, and ways?

3. Knowing about the relationships between these ethnic groups. Are the relationships between various groups cooperative and supportive, or are they antagonistic and hostile? Have these relationships existed historically over centuries, over decades, or are they very recent?

Knowing One's Own Identity

Modern-day Americans need to be put in contact with their own identity and their own past and heritage. This is true for adults as well as for children. In sections of this vast nation, with its highly mobile population, individuals have lost contact with their immigrant past or distinctive family ethnicity. In their book, *Ethnic Families in America; Patterns and Variations,* Charles Mindel and Robert W. Habenstein write that there are large numbers of Americans who find it possible to trace their lines of descent to countries such as Germany, Scotland, Wales, England, France, Belgium, Holland, yet who retain little, if any of this European cultural heritage. Their life styles are largely indistinguishable from others of similar socioeconomic classes.

Many Americans are of mixed traditions with various ethnic heritages represented on one side of the family or the other. If they are to recognize and identify the basic heritage and traditions that they hold uniquely as individuals, it is through their family and its heritage that they will find them. Therefore, we must put people in touch with the family context that shaped their personality, identity and self concept. This is as true for teachers as it is for their students.

Where, then, do the school and the curriculum come in? It is in school that the classroom teacher is in the position to redress some of the discrimination and prejudicial treatment that children, who have been identified as different, have experienced. Teachers can set the scene for a child's favorable identification with his or her own family and heritage. Teachers can reduce ethnic self-hatred and increase a child's self-esteem by valuing the heritage and traditions represented by the family and ethnic group from which a child derives its identity and self concept.

The subjects of the curriculum, as well as daily classroom programs offer many opportunities for helping children identify and value their family heritage. For example, the teacher does not need a special occasion or holiday to assign children, at any age level, to interview their grandparents. Children will find their grandparents or older aunts and uncles open and quite willing to recount past experiences and impressions. A new rapport and understanding is forged between the generations in these interviews. The younger person often finds values and practices exist that he or she never recognized or heard articulated, and the older person feels needed and appreciated by the child, the family and the larger society.

Knowing about Other Groups

Not only should we be able to conceptualize and understand our own ethnicity and our own heritage, but we must also be knowledgeable about and sensitive to other groups. Blacks want to explore the many facets of Black ethnic and racial heritage, just as Whites are concerned about the varieties of White ethnic experience. But we must not stop here. We need to develop what some ethnic scholars call "ethnic literacy"—a wider realization and understanding of ethnicity and ethnic groups. This knowledge of, as well as empathy for ethnic diversity is necessary not only for our survival as a nation, but also for America's ability to flourish in a worldwide society.

Ethnic literacy requires understanding of the aspects of ethnicity and understanding of the historical and geographic origins of various groups of people. It is particularly important that the individual know about the ethnic and racial groups living in a specific geographical area or community, since it is likely that at some time he or she will come into contact with members of these groups. When we all share in the values and traditions of a group of people, we give credence and validity to its members. We should be knowledgeable about the size of ethnic populations and the length of time, the number of generations, they have contributed to our nation's history. We tend to forget that some people lived on the American continent long before the European and, more specifically, the Anglo Saxon tradition came to America. Spanish Americans and Native Americans, for example, trace their presence in the Southwest back to the 16th Century and before. Yet we think of this country as a vast, empty land that was filled up and civilized by the Europeans because, until recently, that is how most books in the public schools have portrayed American history.

In recent years, ethnic scholars, among them Carlos Cortes of the University of California at Riverside, have decried the facts that most history books and teaching of U.S. history in our schools give only token recognition to the growth of civilization, industry and development in America prior to the coming of the Europeans. Most history courses ignore the growth of the Native American, Hispanic and Mexican civilizations BEFORE the United States conquest of their territory. We are taught in our American history courses that the flow of civilization in the United States occurred from the East Coast to the West, as we fulfilled our "Manifest Destiny." Now it is urged that we reject this simplistic, ethnocentric approach with which we have taught American history in the past and provide more accurate and authentic information to students at every age and grade level.

Knowing about the Relationship Between Groups

We need to have more extensive knowledge of and empathy for relationships between ethnic and racial groups. Are these relationships cooperative or antagonistic? Has there been a history of domination of one group over the other? Has the hostility and enmity endured over the years in a smoldering, covert fashion, or has it been expressed in riots, lynchings and vigilante behavior such as the Ku Klux Klan during the 1920's and 1930's?

What are the tensions that persist between the ethnic groups? Are they found in the political, economic, social or educational arena? How virulent and detrimental are these tensions and prejudices? Over three decades ago, Max Lerner, observed that members of each new wave of immigrants to this country were assigned the lowliest and most onerous of tasks. The basic pattern was, however, for the immigrants of each new influx in time to be absorbed by the rest, yielding the role of strangeness in turn to the still later comers. Most of these new comers to America moved up the social and economic ladder to become integrated into the society and its economic largess. (Lerner, 1957)

A more recent study of ethnic group tensions and the process of ethnic succession in business, the professions and in politics was carried out by the Institute for Pluralism and Group Identity. In the 1970's researchers documented inter-ethnic strife in the Philadelphia schools. This case study was representative of other large city school systems, as well. It was noted that there were other confrontations than just the white-black disputes found in the headlines in the daily papers. We began to recognize group collisions between Blacks and Jews over teaching positions in the New York schools, between Newark's Black and Italian groups for political power, between Chicanos and Blacks in Los Angeles over leadership in poverty programs, and among Protestant, Catholics and Jews over issues of abortion, pornography, and government aid to parochial schols. We are aware that racial and ethnic strains have been a source of friction and even violence in our communities. (Elazar and Friedman, 1976)

Not until the latter 1970's had representatives of ethnic and women's groups, expressed their feelings in open, loud and angry voices. In the past they were more likely to voice their hurt and confusion in the privacy of their own homes or to confide in fellow sympathizers. But all this has been changing dramatically as first Blacks, with the Black Awareness Movement, then Chicanos, Native Americans and all sorts of women's groups, are demonstrating publicly and using the media to state their messages for equal opportunity and recognition. Moreover, new conceptions of ethnic and gender relationships are forming as electronic communications make the world what one linguist called "a whispering gallery." Where are we moving? We are moving into a pluralistic society that dictates pluralistic education for all its public schools.

Pluralism Means Recognition of Ethnicity, Gender, and Power in the Curriculum

It is time public education recognized that the movements for integration, ethnic heritage, bilingualism and women's rights are vitally linked. Each of these crusades represents important aspects of American life, but none by itself can bring about the changes needed in our democratic system. Joining together in a coalition that works toward the shared interest of all parties can accomplish much more.

The movement for bilingual and bicultural education represents another major effort by the educational system to respond to student diversity. Bilingual education is not only a controversial political issue, but it also poses some serious philosophical problems for most traditional educators. The standard educational philosophy for the last century has been that English is the language of America, and to permit the day-to-day use of any other language in the system especially at the elementary school level was doing the student a disservice. To allow the student to maintain his or her native language, if it was other than English, was to diminish the chance of success within the American socioeconomic system. Many stories are told of children who were punished or ridiculed for using their family's native tongue in school. The English-only law that has been passed in several states in recent years has thrown the whole area of bilingual education into turmoil and confusion.

Today, this philosophy of English-as-the-official language is being seriously challenged by the Hispanic community and other ethnic groups who speak languages other than English. Language is one of the strongest psychic bonds; a new language is not learned cognitively like mathematics but is primarily an emotional and perceptual experience. Even if children are able to cope with a new language, they may attribute a higher cultural value to the classroom than to their home culture and mother tongue, to the detriment of their self esteem.

It was the landmark case of Lau v. Nichols in 1974, brought on behalf of Chinese children in San Francisco, that provided the legal mandate for bilingual-bicultural education programs across the country. It is hardly coincidental in a nation as pluralistic and multicultural as ours that one ethnic group (Chinese Americans in San Francisco) should obtain a major Supreme Court decision that has benefited and promoted bilingual education for non-English speaking children everywhere in the country.

The preeminent sociolinguist, Joshua Fishman, argues that monolingual and monocultural education is artificial, particularly if we have one world in mind. Fishman tell us that the world is not unifiable on the basis of cultural monisms. We all hold multiple group memberships. Through multilingual and multicultural education we can help children learn about the rich diversity of human groups, those interlocking and simultaneous loyalties and memberships. (Fishman, 1976)

Current bilingual education in the United States is based on two major premises. The first is that there are important psychological supports in the native language itself and in the attendant identification of culture, family values and sense of belonging to one's ethnic group. To destroy the language is to isolate the child from his family and inheritance. The second premise is that the child who does not speak English as he or she enters public school

is disadvantaged in learning subject matter taught only in English. Therefore, subject matter should be taught in English and in other native languages so that the student does not fall behind in content while learning English as a second language.

One example of the commitment and concern of major city school systems to multi-lingual and multicultural education is demonstrated in this quotation taken from the annual report to the citizens of Denver, by the Denver Public Schools. In a colorful, photo-filled, four page newsletter put out by the Public Information and Services Office of the Denver Public Schools, a feature statement proclaims "As one of the nation's large urban centers, Denver serves one of the most heterogeneous populations in the State of Colorado. The nearly 60,000 students represent an international spectrum of 74 countries and 85 languages. The Denver Public Schools celebrates this rich diversity as a unitary system knowing that it in no way takes away from the educational process. On the contrary, it adds to the wealth of knowledge and promotes human understanding". (Denver Public Schools, 1989)

Just as the Denver Public Schools has done, a large number of school systems are using multilingual and bilingual education to meet the needs of their non-English speaking students. But the value and cost of these programs are being hotly debated within communities, among various ethnic groups, and within the faculty of school systems—and Denver is not excepted. The main problem areas are:

1. the strong feeling that English is the only proper language for Americans to speak; reinforced by recently passed laws that only English be recognized as the official language of the state.
2. the fear that the cost of bilingual and multilingual education is higher than monolingual education;
3. the concerns that those faculty members who are not multilingual will be dismissed from their school positions; or tensions and conflict will arise between cliques of staff members over linguistic rivalries.

In addition to bilingual-bicultural objectives, pluralistic education also encompasses issues central to the women's movement. Through the years, our educational system has reinforced the sex role stereotypes embraced by society at large. Most teachers, women and men, have willingly perpetuated these stereotypes as they were represented in everything from children's picture books to textbooks on history, civics and even mathematics. Today, addressing identity conflicts and vocational goals of both women and men in our society is as much a part of pluralistic education as in multilingualism and ethnic group affiliation.

Early childhood educators have reiterated that role expectations are communicated to children early in life. One can find two-year-olds who know what activities and tools are "appropriate" for men and for women. Children observe the adults around them, the roles portrayed on television, then examples of what men and what women do in their storybooks. Children are socialized early to the role models of our cultural stereotypes where masculinity denotes power and hence success, while femininity is usually tied to roles that have little power or status. Men go out to the world of work and women stay home, shielded and sequestered.

We are now in a period of major changes and a new awareness of the myriad possibilities for both women and men. Everyone, but especially teachers, needs to revise their thinking about the roles we are teaching our children to fulfill. Parents, as well as teachers, are recognizing that gender stereotypes are among the prejudices that stunt children's growth and limit their capacity to deal with our complex contemporary society. Therefore, discrimination in all forms—discrimination on the basis of race, class or gender robs the individual of a positive self image and drains the society of valuable human potential. When we deal with differences in the educational process, whether they be ethnic, linguistic, cultural or gender differences, we are recognizing the need for pluralistic education and the role pluralism plays in the curriculum, in the educational materials we use and in the values and attitudes that teachers hold. Elementary school teachers in particular, working with young children as they form their values and attitudes toward society, can have an impact upon the future of a culturally pluralistic America.

Tips for Pluralistic Teaching

The following suggestions and strategies should be useful to teachers working with students of culturally diverse backgrounds. These teaching tips, followed by some cautions, will enrich the pluralistic and multicultural nature of the classroom and provide the background for genuine pluralistic education.

1. Learn each child's name, first and last, using the pronunciation the child's family would use. If pronouncing the name is difficult, practice it before class. Do not be reluctant to ask the child's parents to help you learn the accurate and authentic way to say an unfamiliar name. For too long we have been Anglicizing children's names to the point of destroying their self-image and positive sense of family pride. Names like Culberto become "Joe" and Refugia turns into "Ruth." Parents cherish the names they give their children. Often, the name is part of a family heritage and tradition. Teachers should be continually aware of this fact and make a practice of calling each child by his or her given name.

2. If the children in your class or group come from families that speak languages other than English, learn some phrases, sayings or expressions in those languages and use them in the classroom whenever possible. If none of your students speak a foreign language choose a language of your preference and use some phrases from it in your classroom.

3. Try to provide written materials—storybooks, newspapers, magazines, letters or numbers—or label objects in the room in languages other than English. Discuss these materials and labels, integrating them appropriately into the assignments and lessons for reading, math, social science, art and music.

4. Learn about holidays and festivals that are unique to the ethnic groups represented by your pupils, and take advantage of the activities in your curriculum to reflect these special days. For example, ask parents about special Mexican holidays if you have children of Mexican American background. Jewish holidays, Muslim festivals and Japanese or Chinese or Southeast Asia celebrations provide other opportunities for exploring diverse cultures. Ask parents how these holidays and festivals are celebrated by ethnic communities in the United States.

5. If you know that parents of your children speak and read a language other than English, send notes and announcements home to parents in both languages. Someone from the community can help you with the translations. Send the bilingual notices to all parents, including those who speak only English, so everyone will be aware of your attitudes and thoughtfulness.

Relationship Between Bilingualism, Ethnicity, Integration, The Women's Movement And Pluralistic Teaching

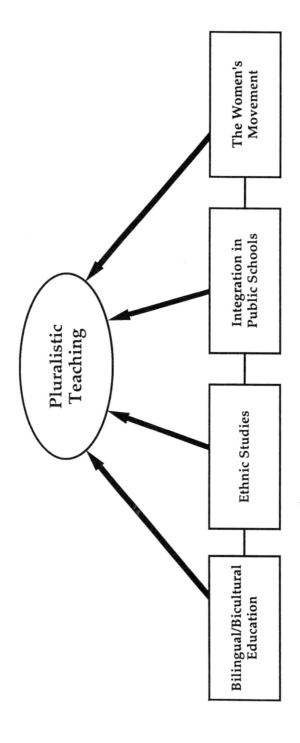

6. Whenever possible, integrate other languages and cultural customs into your daily program, especially in music and art activities. Have the children learn songs in different languages. Find posters, fine art and folk art of a variety of cultures and ethnic groups and display them in your classroom. Plan arts and crafts activities that represent the cultural and ethnic diversity in American society, as well as photos of men and women in diverse activities and nurturing roles.

7. Sometimes disruptive behavior and stereotyping may accompany the use of particular words or language. Impress upon your students that a child's language or dialect is as perfect a linguistic system and as valid a means of communication as the teacher's standard English. Make it a practice to continually demonstrate your respect for other cultures, other languages and other peoples' customs and traditions.

8. When feasible, use parents as consultants, volunteer assistants and sources of expertise and support. Encourage the children to invite their parents to contribute to school programs and to your classroom activities. Make parents feel your classroom is open for them to provide demonstrations of their talents and expertise. For example, as you begin to notice interesting and perhaps unique traditions and customs that might enhance the activities in the classroom, send out little feelers to the children involved, such as "My, I would like to know more about that." Or, "Would your father, (brother), (sister), be available to tell us about that?" You will be surprised how these remarks, if expressed sincerely and with genuine interest, will bring rapid response from the children and their families.

    As you receive responses to your initial overtures, schedule class time for your resource people. Give careful thought to the optimum time for a presentation, both for the guest and for the children in the classroom. This may require that you manipulate the school schedule, but generally the results are worth the trouble you take. For instance, think about when the children will be most receptive and attentive to a visiting resource person. This is usually not the last half-hour in the afternoon, or just before the lunch period.

    Prepare your class in advance. Do not suggest to the parent, "Just drop by when it is convenient." Make both the resource person and the children feel that this is an important event. Consider follow-up activities. The resource person will feel you really care and that he or she has something important to contribute to the learning situation. The children will recognize the contribution to their program, as well.

9. Consider using audio-visual aids with and for the parent or resource person. Recording the event is very valuable; the tape can be played back—audio or video—for reference and reinforcement later. Usually a classroom resource person has no objection to having the presentation tape-recorded or even video-taped. But do ask beforehand whether you may do so. The resource person is usually flattered that you consider the material so important that you wish to record it for later use. Many resource persons like to utilize audio-visual aids themselves, particularly slide projectors, tape recorders and video cassette (VCR) equipment. Try to arrange to have the equipment on hand in your classroom if the resource person isn't supplying his or her own media materials.

10. Remember to follow up and expand the information and experiences the children have received from parents and classroom guests. Discussions, writing short stories, drawing pictures, making a mural, collages, diorama, writing thank-you notes, dramatization, putting on student programs, playback or recorded materials made during the occasions—all of these are valuable follow-up techniques to the parent or resource person's presentation. Do not overlook contrasts and comparisons of opinions, ways of acting, customs, traditions, languages, foods and clothing. Our value system encourages fair and open discussions. By allowing comparisons to develop, children can learn and grow in a non-judgmental climate.

11. It is also essential in the pluralistic classroom climate to maintain a non-sexist attitude about curriculum materials and activities. A new awareness has pervaded schools and classrooms during recent years that heightens sensitivity of teachers, parents and the students, as well, to gender biased textbooks and other curricular materials. Teachers no longer ask girls to sit and watch as the boys move furniture and carry about books and other objects in the classroom. Nor are girls directed to "clean-up" while boys are allowed to continue to play.

One teacher put it this way:

I used to remark about the children's clothing frequently. I did this to help them to become observant of themselves and each other, to develop color sense, and to generally enhance their self-images. I used to be careful to say that girls were pretty and boys were handsome. When I became aware of sexism, I began to examine what I was saying to the children. Instead of "pretty" and "handsome" I used words that connoted comfort and function. "Short sleeves are cool and comfortable for today, David." "Those overalls are great for climbing, Nell." "I like the color combination you chose today, Peter." Just by changing the ways I looked at the children's clothes, I was influencing their attitudes towards appearance without diminishing their pleasure in color or denying them a special bit of attention, and my comments were far more sincere, not hackneyed cliches like looking handsome or pretty. (B. Sprung, 1974, p. 39)

Some Cautions for the Teacher

Teachers should also be aware of some of the pitfalls or problems they may encounter in drawing on parents and resource persons in the community. Here are some cautions you should keep in mind.

1. If you recognize an inflammatory situation in your community or school, think twice before you invite participants in the controversy into your classroom. If you wish to study the problem area as part of the curriculum, try to choose knowledgeable but neutral figures associated with the event. You might even want to postpone discussions and presentations for a later date when things have cooled off. You need not avoid the controversy, but discretion and careful analysis of an explosive issue will determine optimum timing for its inclusion in the classroom program during the school year.

2. Another common pitfall is the "queer people with quaint customs" syndrome. Bringing the customs, traditions and preferences of the children's families or the neighborhood setting into the school can provide enriching and rewarding experiences if adroitly and empathetically handled. But without careful planning the program can reinforce ethnocentric prejudices and actually damage some children psychologically. A colonialistic, condescending presentation can be devastating and rejection-filled for the children who are affiliated with the ethnic, national or racial minority group you are studying. It defeats the very purpose of the cross-cultural, cross-racial or multiethnic experience if the activities are allowed to take on the condescending "aren't they quaint" demeanor that at times does characterize simulated fiestas, luaus or other ceremonies.

3. In order to avoid a demeaning and potentially harmful experience for the children, locate cooperative parents and become as well informed as possible about the ethnic group or groups involved. Do not be snoopy, but genuinely interested in the traditions, history and meaning of the group's practices. The aspects of ethnicity discussed and detailed in Chapter One, are a good starting point to help you inquire in a knowledgeable way about the little-known ethnic group. This takes time, energy and a distinct desire to reach out to others, but it is absolutely necessary for worthwhile and effective interaction. The superficial "tourist approach" (just passing through to see the natives) produces the "queer people with quaint customs" syndrome; genuine concern and commitment to the needs and views of others produces valuable intercultural understanding.

4. Sometimes even when you have carefully planned the use of parents from the ethnic groups in the community, unexpected problems arise during or after the activity or visit to the school. Before you jump in with a quick solution, stand back and analyze the situation. Sometimes the tension resolves itself and proves to be only a temporary misunderstanding. If the situation continues to look threatening, try to provide a neutral setting where grievance and misunderstandings can be aired and problems openly discussed. In this atmosphere, a resolution can usually be achieved.

5. Be aware of your personal biases. Have you been allowing specific children, a group of boys, or certain girls to dominate the classroom? Do you have hidden preferences for choosing boys and allowing them to take over the discussions or bid for the most prestigeful positions or activities? (One reason that boys get more of the teacher's attention is that they just demand it). Is your classroom segregated by sex? Do children march between classes and to various activities in sex-segregated lines or divide into work and play teams by gender? How can you subtly but forcefully help children to be more pluralistic in their choices of others to interact with in the classroom and on the playground?

Summary

In this chapter we discussed the importance of personal and group identity within a distinctly American heritage. Schools can no longer deny ethnicity and the pluralistic nature of our society which includes race, class and gender equity. Every aspect of the curriculum must reflect and address ethnic groups represented in American culture. In short, we need to educate for ethnic literacy.

Ethnic literacy can be instilled through pluralistic education which is characterized by:

1. knowledge and understanding of one's own heritage, background and family history, of whatever ethnic and racial makeup it may be;

2. knowledge and understanding of the heritage of other groups that make up the pluralistic culture of Americans;

3. knowledge and understanding of the relationships among people who make up the ethnic groups in the United States, both historically and currently.

Pluralistic education represents the goals of a coalition of movements, including integration, bilingualism, ethnic and the women's movement. This chapter concluded with some suggestions for implementing pluralistic education—race, class and gender—in education in the elementary school classroom.

References

Cortes, C. E. "The Societal Curriculum: Implications for Multiethnic Education." in J. A. Banks (ed.) *Education in the 80's.* (pp. 24–32) Wash. D.C. National Education Association, 1981.

Banks, J. and Banks, C. *Multicultural Education: Issues and Perspective.* Allyn and Bacon, 1989.

Denver Public Schools. 1987–1988 *Report to the Community.* Denver, 1989.

Elazar, D. and Friedman, M. *Moving Up; Ethnic Succession in America.* New York: Institute for Pluralism and Group Identity, 1976.

Fishman, J. *Bilingual Education; An International Sociological Perspective.* Rowley, Mass. Newbury House, 1976.

Lerner, Max. *America as a Civilization.* New York: Simon and Shuster, 1957.

Mindel, C. H. and Habenstein, R. W., Editors *Ethnic Families in America; Patterns and Variations.* N.Y.: Elsevier Publ. Co. 1976: 3d Edition 1988 with R. Wright Jr.

Sprung, B. *Guide to Non-Sexist Early Childhood Education.* New York: Women's Action Alliance, 1974.

3

The Impact of Race, Class and Gender on Diversity in Education

A decade ago hardly anyone was concerned with ethnicity, let alone personal heritage and gender. In recent years, though, a dramatic change has occurred, boosted, some believe, by Alex Haley's *Roots* when it first appeared as a book, and then as a serialized television program. Suddenly, ethnic and gender awareness were not just for minorities, not just for Blacks, Mexican Americans, Native Americans or White ethnics. Every person has an ethnic identity, a heritage that shapes his or her attitudes, values, tastes, habits and choices in everyday life.

People differ in the degree to which they recognize their own ethnic identity and in their awareness of how ethnicity affects their day-to-day lives. Furthermore, many people do not realize that their ethnicity changes with the passage of time, with geographic location, with upward or downward social mobility and with their professional and social contacts. Ethnic educators like to say that ethnic identities are the locations people choose for themselves on the ethnic map.

To illustrate the dynamics of ethnic and gender identity, let us consider the example of one second-grade teacher in a Midwestern American public school. Before she married her husband, a Greek by birth who became an American citizen in his early twenties, Mary was Irish American and proud of it. She had learned of the traditions and special customs of her Irish mother and grandmother from both of them and she especially enjoyed celebrating St. Patrick's Day in her hometown, participating in the parade and the "wearing of the Green." But after she was married and accompanied her husband to his family village in the south of Greece, she became more and more interested in learning how to cook the new foods she had enjoyed so much with his family. Further, her Greek in-laws had bestowed upon Mary lovely clothes, blouses and skirts that were hand embroidered, as well as linens and other family heirlooms. Mary treasured this fine folk art, both clothing and artifacts, and brought the pieces back home to America.

After a number of years, Mary and her husband moved to a city in the Southwest. She found a teaching position in an elementary school and her husband started a new business. They met new acquaintances through their careers and in their new neighborhood. Now when people met Mary she was introduced to them by her married name, Mary P_____ and people just assumed she was of Greek America descent. There happened to be none of her family or friends in this city who knew her maiden name or original Irish heritage. Mary did not feel upset about this because she rather enjoyed being considered Greek American. She wore her lovely Greek blouses on special occasions and cooked the Greek foods she had learned to make when in Greece. People in her new neighborhood and school just assumed she had been born into this Greek heritage and never questioned her ethnic identity. Moreover, Mary's assumption of the Greek American ethnicity was facilitated by her gender and the social custom in the United States of women taking on their husband's family name when they marry and dropping their maiden name. Additionally, Mary's first name lent itself to her Greek-sounding last name. People who had not known her from childhood just surmised that she was of Greek ethnic background and Mary did not choose to change their impression. Thus, ethnic identity can be a dynamic force in a person's life, affected by such variables as the passage of time, social events such as marriage, geographical location, travel experiences and customs surrounding gender and self identity.

Let us review definitions of the terms discussed in Chapter One, ethnicity, ethnic identity and ethnic group to reinforce their meanings. By ETHNICITY, we mean a sense of peoplehood, a sense of commonality derived from kinship patterns that include a shared historical past, common experiences, religious affiliation, a common linguistic heritage, as well as shared values, attitudes, perceptions, more and folkways. ETHNIC IDENTITY we have defined as the personal dimension of ethnicity or how one identifies one self. A person is ethnic if he or she chooses to be. An individual may choose among ethnic preferences, whether these ethnic affiliations are inherited or acquired by marriage—as the way Mary in our previous account chose her ethnicity. It is not unusual, as in Mary's case, for a woman in our society to marry and take on an ethnic name. Then she makes a concerted effort to learn how to cook the ethnic dishes of her acquired heritage and to become familiar with the customs, traditions, festivals and holidays of that heritage. Her friends are shocked and surprised one day when they find out by accident that she was not born into, but married into, her current ethnic group.

An ETHNIC GROUP is a group of people within a larger society which has a common ancestry and history, may speak a native tongue other than English and may practice customs and traditions which reflect their ancestry. An ETHNIC MINORITY GROUP is an ethnic group that has unique physical characteristics which make its members easily identifiable and may subject them to discrimination and prejudice in the broader society.

The Persistence of Ethnicity

Once the individual recognizes and declares a specific affiliation, this heritage is often carried on through the family tradition from generation to generation. True, the customs and folkways may undergo variation and mutation, but the core of ethnic identity is still recognizable. Ethnic scholars, particularly sociologists, have noted this, not only in examining American ethnicity, but in transnational contexts as well.

Since the 1960s more and more sociologists have been studying and researching ethnic groups in American society. One of the most well known of these studies, *Beyond the Melting Pot,* (1963) was undertaken by Nathan Glaser and Daniel Moynihan, and it looked at Blacks, Puerto Ricans, Jews, Italians and Irish in New York City. Glaser and Moynihan found that ethnic groups, because of their distinctive historical experiences, their cultures and skills, the time of their arrival and the economic situation they met in America, developed distinctive economic, political, and cultural patterns. As the old traditions and customs faded away, new ways shaped by the distinctive experiences of life in America were formed and a new identity arose. For example, Italian Americans might share little with Italians in Italy, but in America they were a distinctive group that maintained itself, was identifiable, and gave a sense of support and belonging to those who were identified with it. However, stereotyping and prejudice also accompanied those who claimed Italian American heritage. Just as these discriminatory attitudes haunt other ethnic and ethnic minority groups in New York City and the major cities in our country.

Timroel

25 A

Compare this description of Italian Americans in New York City with the observations of British race relations authorities about West Indians in Britain. These British sociologists say that when West Indians first came to Britain as migrant workers in the 1950s, it seemed to many white Britons that they were Black Englishmen and Englishwomen. Their own group interest and identities were often suppressed by their needs to make a living. But in recent years both these West Indian immigrants and their children, are demonstrating more open hallmarks of their ethnic affiliation. For example, in Jamaica, Rastafarianism was a quasi-religious cult which called for a back-to-Africa movement. In Britain, Rasta is now the means of emotional and physical support to a generation of black youths who seek roots. (Ballard and Driver, 1977)

It is important to note that West Indians are characterized as an ETHNIC MINORITY GROUP in Britain, while Italian Americans are usually designated as an ETHNIC GROUP in America. While it may seem that the persistence of West Indian ethnicity is attributable to racial discrimination, British sociologists make a strong case for the positive vitality of ethnic minority affiliation, emphasizing that many ethnic groups exhibit the desire to reinforce their ethnic identity in a diverse society.

The persistence of ethnic identification in contemporary pluralistic societies is due to both negative and positive factors. When the primary reason for group affiliation is hostility from the majority group, it is inevitable that ethnicity seems more to confine and constrict the individual than to provide opportunities and enhance the quality of life. But people are usually drawn to ethnic identification because of the advantages it offers. The ethnic group can be a buffer between the individual and the broader society; individuals use ethnicity as a filter for forming their opinions, tastes, values and habit patterns. Ethnic affiliations also help organize social, economic, political, and religious interaction, both among individuals and among groups.

The Social Construction of Ethnic and Gender Identity

In exploring the concept of ethnic indentity, we inevitably encounter questions about the "reality" of the social world in which the individual exists. It seems appropriate, then, to introduce the theory of the social construction of reality and to apply it to the meaning of ethnicity and ethnic and gender identity. The leading theorists on the topic of the social construction of reality are Peter Berger and Thomas Luckmann, whose ideas and insights will help clarify the significance of the social construction of ethnic and gender identity.

Berger and Luckmann contend that the reality of everyday life presents itself to us as a world we share with others. We share a common sense about what is reality and, therefore, our everyday life is characterized by a taken-for-granted reality. But human beings are unique among living creatures, for they can experience and exist in several provinces of meaning or taken-for-granted realities. These can be enclaves within the paramount reality.

The theater provides an excellent metaphor for coexisting realities. To this point Berger and Luckmann tell us:

> The transition between realities is marked by the rising and falling of the curtain. As the curtain rises, the spectator is "transported into another world" with its own meanings and an order that may or may not have much to do with the order of everyday life. As the curtain falls, the spectator "returns to reality." (Berger and Luckmann, 1966; 25)

So it can be with an individual's ethnic identity. Within the ethnic group, the taken-for-granted world calls for conduct, use of language, referents, mutual affinities and antipathies that are implicit and unspoken. These ways are shared with others of the same ethnic and racial affiliations. The same individual functions within the majority society in the taken-for-granted reality of the supermarket, the street traffic or the daily newspaper. Common habit patterns take over to guide conduct. A person pays the price posted and does not bargain with the cashier at the supermarket; goes on the green light and halts on the red light, not chancing the traffic just because no cars are apparent; and comprehends the news story on the front page about rising food prices. We accept and function within cultural continuities even from childhood.

Each day, young children leave their home, where they function in the taken-for-granted reality of their ethnic affiliations, to go to the majority society (Anglo-oriented) school. Children perform their roles as students in the school for approximately six hours each day, adhering to the shared meanings of the broader American society, standing in lines (often one for girls and another for boys) as they move from room to room; reading their basal readings in English; passively listening to teachers' directions and discussions filled with references to the general American heritage; joining in the celebration of the holidays of the majority group—Christmas, Easter, Valentine's Day, Halloween. Many children just as docilely and unquestioning return home, sometimes to "their section of town", to resume life in the ethnic group with its own cultural patterns, traditions, perhaps even a different language for the rest of the day and night. This represents one aspect of the social construction of ethnic identity. Reality is being a marginal person living with two everyday realities, one at school and one at home. We have only recently begun to recognize that people frequently occupy several provinces of cultural meaning, and that this is not necessarily deleterious, yet some teachers still declare that, if a child's ethnic affiliations are not those of the majority society, there are bound to be cultural differences, and to educators of the majority society, these differences mean cultural DISADVANTAGES.

Our view of reality and of the world helps us to make sense of our experiences. We interpret social events in light of the social meanings we attach to them. Here our ethnic identification and ethnic affiliation come forth to interpret the meaning of everyday occurrences.

For example, if in recent times you asked a young child of majority group affiliations, or predominantly Anglo ethnic backgrounds, "Who are you?" the child might reply, "I am Mary Smith," or "I am Johnnie Jones." But if you asked the same question of a young Black in the urban ghetto of New York or Trenton, New Jersey, you might receive the reply, "I am BLACK and BEAUTIFUL!"

Another incident will illustrate the stigmatizing aspects of ethnic identity. Consider the remark, heard frequently in some middle and high school circles, "Watch out, buddy, or he will JEW you down." Just a remark, a gentle caution to many teenagers, but an ethnic insult, a real put-down for a Jewish youngster. An American Jewish teenager's reaction to this offhand remark was the following: "When I first heard that statement in the corridor one day, it burned in my ears, and I could not forget it for weeks and weeks. I took it as a personal insult!" So subtle is our ethnic identity, so unconsciously do we carry it, that when everyday speech, common talk, penetrates to our ethnic consciousness, we are caught off guard.

While we are discussing the social construction of ethnic identity, we should also examine the meanings of this concept for the social construction of gender identity. An individual is socialized and enculturated into assuming the roles and behavior of the society that is considered proper for one's sex—male or female. We internalize behavior that is considered appropriate for boys or for girls. The following anecdote about pre-schoolers in the "housekeeping corner" clearly illustrated this. Two boys are playing by the child-sized sink at one end of the "housekeeping" area of a neighborhood early childhood center. They appear to be gathering dishes to set the table for a snack. One boy reaches over to a cardboard box filled with dress-up clothes and pulls out an apron. He attempts to tie the apron around his waist, but seems to be having a problem getting it to stay on. The teacher's attention is attracted to the two boys when they begin to argue quite loudly. One boy is jeering at the other, pointing his finger and shouting "Dannie is like a GIRL; he is trying to wear girls' clothes." Dannie is loudly disaffirming his actions and stamping on the apron.

The teacher goes over to the two boys and scolds them for the disruptive behavior. She takes the apron away from the "housekeeping corner" and reprimands Dannie for trying to "dress up" in an outfit that girls wear, as the little boy slinks away and goes over to his table, puts his head down on his arms and hides his face in shame. The teacher could have handled the situation more adroitly, if she had calmed the two boys by remarking that both men and women wear aprons to protect their good clothing. Sometimes men wear aprons when they cook or barbecue, or if they are working on certain types of machinery and need to hold small parts in the pockets of the apron, so aprons are not just an item of clothing for girls, boys can wear them, too.

Primary and Secondary Socialization

Every person is born into a human group which shapes or socializes him or her during childhood. (Mead, 1934). Through socialization, social constructions (in other words, social reality) are internalized by the individual. Hence, the individual's self-perceptions and identity are being formed through his or her encounters with everyday life.

Berger and Luckmann state that significant others (often parents) interpret the meanings of experience in the social world for the child. "Thus the lower-class child not only absorbs a lower-class perspective of the social world, he absorbs it in the idiosyncratic coloration given it by his parents. They point out that the lower-class child will not only come to inhabit a world greatly different from the upper-class child, but may do so in a manner quite different fron the lower-class child NEXT DOOR (Berger and Luckmann, 1966; 131)

This idea applies not only to social class membership, but to ethnic affiliation as well. Ethnic identity helps explain the vast differences in the individual's perceptions of the social world across class lines. Ethnic identity also give us a more accurate understanding of why an individual might interpret social reality in so many diverse ways. Primary socialization, as these sociologists term enculturation, the internalizing of values, attitudes, preferences and habit patterns in the early years of life, has the greatest impact on the individual. All secondary socializaton must be filtered and made to fit within the social construction of reality internalized during primary socialization.

The diverse impact of primary socialization is evident in the case of two brothers reared in a large, economically disadvantaged Mexican American family. Their family lived in the barrio of a small town in an agricultural area of the Southwest. At the age of five or six, most of the 21 children in the family were put to work in the fields, picking beans or sugar beets for a few pennies an hour to contribute to the family's earnings. The usual pattern for Mexican American boys and girls in the area was to drop out of school at twelve or thirteen and go to work in the fields permanently. Schooling was transitory, usually taught by English-speaking teachers to these Spanish-speaking children in a separate school, labeled the "Mexican School." Classrooms were crowded with up to 60 children in each, using poor, rundown facilities and old textbooks. When it came time for the two brothers to leave this elementary school and go on to the high school, the older of the two boys dropped out, but the younger brother persisted. He stayed on in the secondary school, learning English, excelling in mathematics and finally graduating.

The older brother, with only an elementary school education, continued to work in the fields, married at seventeen and had many children, perpetuating the lifestyle of his parents. The younger of the two boys went to work at numerous jobs that led him to travel about the Southwest. He earned enough money as an oil-well rigger to set aside a sum to go to college. First a degree in teaching mathematics, then an opportunity to apply for law school through a minority scholarship program, led him to a professional career. As a successful lawyer, he returns to the small town's barrio area to visit his brother and others of his family. The gulf grows wider and wider between the social realities of these two men. Born into the same objective social structures, each chose selected aspects, selected social constructions. Each man interpreted his social reality in ways that rendered their present situations in life and their social constructions vastly different.

These brothers' interpretations of social reality were influenced by ethnic group members and ethnic identity as much as by social class. On the one hand, the older brother saw the social constructions of his world as limiting his life space and his opportunities. In his secondary socialization he internalized the "institution-based sub world" and the role-specific knowledge of the society. He accepted the "tacit understandings, evaluations, and affective colorations" of the broader American society. (Berger and Luckmann, 1969, 138)

The older brother acquiesced to majority Americans' stereotype of the Mexican American, a stereotype that says he is dumb, poor, inept, passively accepting his lot, unable to extricate himself from the culture of poverty. Objective social reality had a different effect on the younger brother. His reaction was to strive for upward social mobility, to appropriate new opportunities (the scholarships for Mexican Americans), to actualize his ambitions for higher status in American society.

Biographies and personal histories constantly reveal how the chance factors of everyday life can affect each individual differently. A teacher, sensitized and aware of the crucial nature of ethnic identity, can often exploit the idiosyncratic nature of social reality, providing that catalyst, that spark to help the minority child in his or her classroom to learn and achieve.

Primary Socialization and Ethnic Affiliation

Often, growing up in the ethnic enclave, ghetto or barrio socializes children into the belief that all the world is Mexican American or Jewish or Italian or Puerto Rican. Teachers must realize that children hold these conceptions quite naturally and logically. Recognizing these limiting lifestyles and constructing teaching and learning experiences that broaden and expand children's conceptions of the social world is vital in a pluralistic society.

An example of the type of primary socialization that lulls a child into believing that most of the existing society that she or he will ever encounter is made of people of the same ethnicity or race as the child, is revealed in this description. A Chinese child from San Francisco states it this way:

> You never thought about anti-Chinese prejudice, it never hit you in person, until you were eleven or twelve and went to junior high school and got called Chink or Chinaman for the first time. The public elementary schools were ninety-five percent Chinese. The teachers were mostly white women and the language was English, of course. But after school let out for the day, you went to Chinese school everyday for two hours to learn to read and write Chinese. (Wolfe. 1969;132)

In some cases, when poverty limits the benefits parents can bestow on their children, group tradition supplies social mechanisms intended to ameliorate the situation. An example of this is found among Puerto Rican and Central American societies. There is a special type of relationship that exists in these heritages, called "godparenthood" or CAMPAD RAZGO. It calls for a person to sponsor a child at baptism and christening to become the child's lifelong godfather or godmother (padrino or madrina). This sponsorship creates a special bond, not only between the adult and the child, but also between the biological parents of the child and the godparents. In this arrangement children can have a number of adults who are deeply attached to them and are concerned about their welfare. Therefore, teachers need to be aware of the significant others in the lives of children. Ethnic group practices and traditions vary widely, and teachers should not assume that their pupils have been exposed to a primary socialization identical to their own.

Primary Socialization and Gender

We have noted previously with the inclusion of several anecdotes the impact of gender—male or female—on self perception and self identity. Teachers need to be aware of the dynamics of sex role behaviors in their classrooms. Too often, as we have described above, a teacher just reproduces the attitudes and values of the majority culture unthinkingly and unwittingly reinforcing the primary socialization of the majority society. In recent years much more research has focused on gender relations in the elementary classrooms, as well as looking at intergroup relations and prejudice reduction. One such study to observe and record gender-related activities of fourth graders was designed and carried out by a highly motivated teacher in the private school where she taught. She noted how often the children in the class, when given a choice, elected to work and play with others of their own sex. In addition to separating themselves into different groups, the girls and boys in this fourth grade class were observed interacting in very different ways.

The researcher commented that much of the boys' play seemed adversarial, combative, almost violent, especially in comparison to the girls' play, which was non-violent, and more affiliative, cooperative, sometimes nurturant and caring. When she asked one boy why he thought the boys played war, he said that it was just more of a "boy thing." Another pupil told her that boys like to play things like army men and GI Joes, but girls like to play with dolls. The researcher characterized these gender differences in play orientations, which she noted extended beyond play activities, into two distinct types. The girls' classroom work and play orientations were labeled caretaking/cooperative; while the boys' classroom work and play orientations were termed adversarial/combative. (Spatig, 1988, pp. 27–45)

There are many other sex-role stereotypes that abound in elementary school classrooms besides "boy-type war games play." We need to recognize these biases and prejudices and work conscientiously to dispel them.

Ethnicity, Social Class, and Gender: Two Accounts

The social climate of a pluralistic society allows for many social constructions and a wide variety of lifestyles, sometimes referred to as "social scripts."

In *Sexual Scripts: The Social Construction of Female Sexuality,* Judith Long Laws and Pepper Schwartz draw on the theories of Berger and Luckmann to analyze one set of social scripts, a term they define as the repertoire of acts and statuses recognized by a social group, together with the rules, expectations and sanctions governing these acts. (Laws and Schwartz, 1977) While their book focuses on sexual scripts, scripts can also spring from racial identity, ethnic identity or social class membership. Scripts are influenced further by age, geographic location, business and job categorization. Individuals can "perform" or carry out their scripts in a number of social contexts. We each belong to a number of social groups and function in various social realities simultaneously. The flexibility of human existence can be more easily examined through some accounts that provide examples of ethnic and gender scripts.

Our subject is a unique and dynamic person who doffs and dons several cultural cloaks as he moves through social reality, his ethnic and racial identity providing much of the script. He is Black. He is tall—six feet, five inches. His dress is that of the successful businessman. His booming voice commands attention. He speaks with excellent diction and grammar, but with a dialect that is just slightly reminiscent of Southern rural Black speech patterns, so that occasionaly in talking he will employ Black speech idioms or refer to the traditions of the Black heritage of the South. "Now you be sure all the good folk are there." This affectation belies the fact that he was born in Brazil and migrated to California, then to New Mexico before he was a teenager. His native language is actually Portuguese, his second language is Spanish. His childhood years were spent in the American Southwest where he received his public schooling. Our subject financed his college education by working for various Hollywood movie stars. His professional position is that of a U.S. government official directing the financial affairs of one of the armed services. He also serves on as an educational advisor and school board member in a major U.S. city.

This highly visible Black executive chooses to adopt the scripts of several differing social constructions. His background of experiences provides him with a secondary socialization that is characterized by the internalization of several scripts, scripts representing upper middle-class White traditions. Our subject, who functions so readily in this type of script, purposefully adapts at times the social constructions of the Black American, in both personal interactions and for public appearances. He uses his blackness in American society to dispel long-held stereotypes of the Black man.

Our next subject is a beautiful, well dressed, and striking Black woman. Her hair and nails are always in perfect condition adding to her finely groomed and tasteful appearance. Her voice and diction is thoroughly standard Midwestern English and her vocabulary is extensive. She is a college professor, author, minister, wife and mother. Her various roles and responsibilities bring her in contact with adults and children of many ethnic and racial backgrounds. Her talents and abilities make her a sought after speaker and consultant. She has managed to blend a wide variety of social and sexual scripts into a lifestyle that carries her across racial, ethnic and gender barriers.

Tips for New Awareness in Our Diverse Society

We know that ethnic group affiliation and gender identity is decisively influenced by what happens in the schools as well as the home. Yet, by the time a child comes to school, he or she has already been socialized into a set of language patterns, values, attitudes, habits and customs which are determined by ethnicity and gender. If the school, however subtly, devalues these characteristics, the child will inevitably have less self-esteem and pride. Since there is a direct relationship between a child's self esteem (or lack of it) and the ability to learn, children who have been made to feel inferior because of their ethnicity or gender will find the learning process more difficult.

Teachers can call upon the concepts of the social construction of ethnic and gender identity and primary and secondary socialization to bring a new awareness in their classrooms and revitalize their teaching. In this chapter we have explored the realms of meaning inherent in belonging to an ethnic group or an ethnic minority group. The conception of social scripts, understood as the repertoire of acts and statuses recognized as valid by a social group, has also contributed to our understanding of ethnic and gender identity.

References

Ballard, R. and Driver, G. "The Ethnic Approach." *New Society.* June, 1977, pp. 543–5.

Barth, Frederick. (editor) *Ethnic Groups and Boundaries.* Boston: Little, Brown, and Co. 1969.

Berger, Peter and Luckmann, Thomas. *The Social Construction of Reality.* New York: Anchor Books, 1966.

Cuzzort, R. P. and King. E. W. *20th Century Social Thought.* 4th edition, Ft. Worth: Holt, Rinehart and Winston, 1989.

Glaser, Nathan and Moynihan, Daniel P. *Beyond the Melting Pot.* second edition, Cambridge: M.I.T. Press, 1970.

Laws, Judith and Schwartz, Pepper. *Sexual Scripts: The Social Construction of Female Sexuality.* Hinsdale Ill. Dryden Press, 1977.

Mead, George. *Mind, Self, and Society.* Univ. of Chicago Press, 1934.

Mindel, Charles and Habenstein, Robert, Editors *Ethnic Families in America: Patterns and Variations.* N. Y. Elsevier, 1976: 3d Edition 1988 with R. Wright Jr.

Spatig, Linda. "Learning To Manage The Heart: Gender Relations in an Elementary Classroom" *Educational Foundations.* Vol. 2, No. 2, Summer, 1988, pp. 27–45.

4

Dealing with Difference in School, Community and Nation

An Encounter in the Teachers' Lounge

The scene is a teacher's lounge in a typical suburban elementary school about lunchtime on a day in the middle of December. Betty Cohen is speaking to her co-teacher, Mary White, of the second-third grade teaching team.

Betty: I will be away this afternoon and all day tomorrow for the inservice training at the University, so remember that the Black Jacks Reading Group has to re-do that ditto sheet assignment from yesterday.

Mary: Oh, right. I will try not to forget. Boy, Betty, you Jewish people have it made! You had a vacation for YOUR holiday in September at the Jewish New Year, and Christmas vacation is not far away, so you get to take off OUR holiday, as well. And now you even get a couple of days for applying for this inservice conference.

Betty: No reply. A pained expression on her face as a rush of breath makes a response of a quizzical "uh-h-h?"

The majority of teachers will confidently tell their students that they do not discriminate or go out of their way to point out differences between people. Yet every day, casual conversations mirror the attitudes of ethnocentric, monocultural America. If teachers truly considered all students the same, if they were aware that they lived and worked in a multicultural, pluralistic society, Mary White would not be envying Betty Cohen for "her" holidays and vacations. The institutionalized racist, religious and sexist biases that subtly support these attitudes would not exist in our schools or in society at large. A major goal of multiethnic and non-sexist education is to change the Anglo-centric and patriarchal orientations of the American school system, including curriculum content and methods of teaching. In its place we should provide teachers and students with cultural and ethnic alternatives, eliminating harmful consequences of direct or indirect slurs on traditions, heritages, and practices which happen to vary from the majority society's ways.

Teachers and administrators are expressing a psychological blindness to ethnicity and race when they say, "We do not have any minorities—Blacks, Hispanics, Native Americans or Asians—in our school, so we do not need to concern ourselves with multicultural or ethnic studies." Ethnic scholars say of these well-intentioned but misguided educators, that they assume ethnic studies are courses to learn about "them," meaning ethnic people of color and that American studies are courses that study "us," meaning Anglo-Americans. We must confront these contradictions in our attitudes about differences, acknowledging that in a pluralistic America, all people and their children are "us."

Start with the Teacher: Who Am I? What Are MY Roots?

In dealing with difference teachers have always found it easier to discuss "others" as strange and unusual people living in far-away lands. Alternatively, they sometimes just ignore difference altogether and act as if there were no diversity among children or among various peoples and nations. But to properly comprehend and become sensitive to differences in the classroom, teachers themselves must have a sense of self identity, an awareness of their heritage and background. One teacher expressed it this way:

Up until now I have to admit that I was never very curious about my family background or ethnicity. I referred to my background as simply being from Brooklyn and left it at that. Both my parents were born and raised in Brooklyn, so I always considered Brooklyn the place from which I originated. There never was too much mentioned about where each side of my family came from, so the ties I would normally feel to a particular ethnic group never arose. Now, though, with my desire to center on how to teach and provide multicultural experiences in the early childhood classroom, I want to trace my own ancestry back so that at least I would know more about my background in order to answer any questions the children might ask me. But perhaps more important is the need I have to feel part of an ethnic group or at least know where my family came from. So now, after some efforts spent in tracing my "roots" I at least can say that I am a mixture of English, Scotch, and German nationalities, whereas before I had no idea about my background at all.

Most of the information I was able to get about my ancestry came from my parents. Only my grandmother on my mother's side is alive today, so the sources are not that readily available. One thing that I found surprising was that I was discussing something with my parents that was rarely spoken of before in our family. They were willing to tell me as much as they knew, yet I had to wonder why we never talked about it before.

This teacher's experience in examining her own ethnicity and heritage is not unique. As our awareness of and interest in our own roots grows, we wonder why we have not delved into our family heritage and background before. Perhaps this is because most Americans have not been very interested in their ethnicity until recent decades, until particularly the late 1970s and the celebration of the Bicentennial Year, 1976, with its emphasis on multicultural America and family roots.

A new awareness of one's ethnicity, one's identity, can be accompanied by heightened feelings of gender awareness and the implications this brings for dealing with difference. From reminiscences of her own school experiences another teacher provides this account:

Our school was a predominantly white school so we did not have many minorities in our classes or in extracurricular activities. But I do have vivid memories of gender differences— for example, the extra curricular activities that were offered for boys and for girls. Girls at our school could join the dance team, cheerleading, pep club, Girls' Task and Line Service Club, volleyball, gymnastics or swimming teams. Every spring girls were involved in a May festival contest for the prettiest queen and her court. This activity was usually sponsored by the business community and turned out to be just a popularity contest. Boys did not have similar types of activities. Boys' extracurricular activities included football, cross country running, baseball, track, basketball and so on. These offerings of extracurricular activities suggest that girls were certainly having a different type of socialization than boys.

My direct experiences with gender differences and their effects on my school career and plans for college came in the science and math classes. I remember that my brother was failing in his math class and his teacher went out of her way to get him extra help. With me, I was just encouraged to forget about trying to do well in my math and science courses. I was told that I was just a GIRL and would never need them anyway, since I was going to be a housewife. I know that today in schools we are trying to change all this, but I think many women were raised the way I was, and still many girls are experiencing these traditional attitudes today, from both male and female teachers.

These teachers describe the experiences that socialized them and shaped the values and attitudes that now influence their teaching. In order to deal effectively with difference in the classroom, teachers need to understand themselves, to know their ethnic identity, to evaluate the cross cultural and gender experiences they had in their childhood in their schooling and with their family; in their teens with their peers; and currently in adulthood with their colleagues, their spouses and their own children. If teachers are to develop a successful multiethnic and non-sexist program in their classroom they need to engage in the type of introspection and self-examination that the two teachers previously quoted have done.

The Need for a World Perspective

But self knowledge in relation to one's family and country is not enough in today's world-wide society. Realistic self-perceptions call for placing one's self in a world perspective and in a global society. People need to identify their relationships to a local, regional, national and now, international milieu. Everywhere we read and we hear that this nation's labor force is vying with workers overseas so that schools in the United States are now competing head-on with schools overseas. Educators are told that this nation must turn out students who not only have the skills to compete with their counterparts in other countries but who also understand other cultures sufficiently to deal effectively with them. Now our schools must respond to transnational events and trends by preparing students to live and work in a global society.

Margaret Mead, the anthropologist, was an outstanding social thinker who made major contributions to envisioning a global culture and a worldwide view of humanity. She wrote: "We have the means of reaching all of earth's diverse peoples and we have the concepts that make it possible for us to understand them, and they now share in a world-wide, technologically propagated culture, within which they are able to listen as well as to talk to us." (*Culture and Commitment,* 1970, p. xvi). Mead pointed out that today we have available to us for the first time on the "Spaceship Earth" examples of the ways people have lived at every period over the last fifty thousand years. In her fieldwork she observed that at the same time the New Guinea native looked at a pile of yams and pronounces them "a lot" because he cannot count them, teams at Cape Kennedy calculate the precise second when an Apollo mission must change its course if it is to orbit around the moon. Just as Margaret Mead was describing the wide technological and cultural diversity of the peoples of the world she was calling our attention to the close proximity of these distinctly different traditions

This "small world" syndrome has come to every community in the United States—if not through the actual settlement of immigrants and refugees from formerly little-known places bringing their customs and language; then through the media, the daily news events covered by television, newspapers and radio. Therefore, it follows logically that the public schools across this nation reflect that ethnic and linguistic diversity of their communities. It only makes good sense, then to take advantage of the pluralistic nature of the local community surrounding the elementary school to teach about multiethnic education in that school.

How a Unique School Deals with Difference in the Classroom

In Denver, Colorado, there is an area of single family homes (some built at the turn of the century) adjacent to the Universty of Denver, where a unique multiethnic primary school enrolling approximately 400 children, ages 4 to 8 years, has recently come into prominence. As new, young families, some from countries and cultures from the far corners of the globe, moved into the more spacious homes of this older residential area, the University Park area began to take on an international, multicultural atmosphere. In recent years languages such as Arabic, Italian, Turkish, Korean could be heard on the streets and in the park areas of the community. The all-white faces of residents were replaced by people of many skin colors, as well as fascinating and colorful dress. The University Park community also attracted local residents of differing ethnic and racial backgrounds, who decided to move there because the local school, University Park Elementary School, was offering such outstanding educational experiences for very young children.

University Park School is truly multicultural, having 26 countries and 17 languages of influence represented among its student population of kindergarten through second grade. The school offers special assistance to these many diverse speakers through its English as a Second Language Program. We have described the multiethnic character of the school neighborhood, but further, University Park is "paired for bussing" with an upper elementary school, grades 3 through 5, that additional increases its diverse school population. Hence, the ethnic composition of University Park is recorded as 38 percent Black; 6 percent Hispanic; 8 percent Asian; 1 percent Native American and 47 percent other ethnic groups. Further, the children come from varying socioeconomic levels. The range is from lower to upper-middle class. Many of the students live in single parent homes. The majority of the remaining population have families where both parents are employed. There is, however, extensive family involvement. The parents' high esteem for the principal and the school staff and its multicultural educational programs find expression in their willingness to volunteer in every classroom, in the library, the computer laboratory, for field trips, art classes, to work in the "Publishing Center" and for special events and school-wide programs, such as the "International Images" project pictured in this volume.

"International Images" evolved from the proposal for a mini-grant written and submitted by the dynamic teacher of the gifted and talented (Grade 1–2, Challenge Classroom) to the local public education coalition. It was an intensive six week integrated interdisciplinary project designed to promote international awareness and appreciation of multicultural arts at the early elementary school level. Organized and implemented by the teacher of the gifted and talented, these multidisciplinary, crosscultural arts activities involved the entire school—all the staff and students. It was led by and centered around a well-known and outstanding Denver artist, Susan West, ceramicist and painter, and mother of two children attending University Park. After presenting slides and discussions to every classroom of children in the school on the development, history and techniques of mural making, the artist and the teaching staff proceeded to have each child create a tile depicting the various countries and cultures they had been studying about in their classes, many of these cultures were represented by the children and their families.

The project covered three months of activities including the discussions, creating and coloring the tiles with the use of special glazes, collecting the tiles from each class and then firing them at the artist's studio. Finally, Susan West, University Park's artist-in-residence designed the tile mural and assembled the tiles on the walls at the entrance of the school, where children, parents, teachers and visitors could view and enjoy this unique expression of "International Images" (See photos p. 52).

Dealing with Difference in the Kindergarten

The impetus and stimulation for this incredible outpouring of effort by educators and parents for teaching about multiculturalism and international perspectives to such young children have been an ongoing commitment at University Park for a number of years, now. It is displayed on every corridor wall and especially in the areas of the school's kindergartens, where both of these early childhood teachers, specialize in dealing with differences, global education, and crosscultural perspectives for five-year-olds.

They begin the school year with the theme of "friendship" and the ideas that the world is an interesting place because of difference, yet it is our similarities that tie us together as human beings. "This makes dealing with difference a matter of seeing that differences are all right," notes one University Park kindergarten teacher. "We give children a global feeling from the beginning by studying a different country each week, along with learning a different letter of the alphabet each week. I provide an artifact, or song, game, or some words for each country we study." And a visitor to the kindergartens at University Park cannot help but notice and be impressed by the wide-ranging internationalism displayed in every corner of the rooms—signs in many written languages—Hindi, Arabic, Greek, as well as English; photos, drawings, ceramics, clothing, objects d'art of every description to instill global awareness. Parents are an intimate and essential part of this kindergarten curriculum for global awareness and multicultural education. Children are assigned "homework" every weekend which involves activities with their families to promote research and project development on the current topics and themes in the kindergarten classroom.

These kindergarten teachers assert that children in their classes learn that they are not powerless to do something vital on a worldwide scale. Each spring the year-long activities on global awareness and learning are culminated by the creation of a quilt to which each child contributes and that parents assist in assembling. The quilt is raffled off and the money raised is donated to help alleviate the hunger of children worldwide, impressing upon the University Park kindergartners that they can make a difference in the world.

The English and the Many-Other-Languages Classroom

The English-as-a-Second Language (ESL) teacher of the University Park staff would rather be known as a teacher of "biliterate" students. She says, "most of our students are 'biliterate'; they are learning to read and write in their home language and in English." Her classroom and the adjacent corridor area are overflowing with the internationalism and the crosscultural atmosphere that reflects her educational philosophy and methods for teaching children that speak many different languages and represent a myriad of cultures—Farsi, Arabic, Korean, Vietnamese, Laotian, Hmong, Cantonese, Cambodian, Turkish, Greek, Italian,—and on around the globe. She encourages these children, most of them from recently arrived refugee families, to learn in both their mother tongue and in English. Using parents, siblings, family members and international students from the nearby University of Denver, this dedicated ESL teacher brings her pupils from their assigned classrooms for periods of time in the ESL room for specialized instruction in science, social studies and mathematics. She uses many ways of communicating, learned over her twenty-four years of experience in crosscultural, international and multilingual teaching in the United States and abroad. Her techniques include use of flashcards, charts, games, music, artwork and media materials, as well as the many human resources she attracts to her fascinating classroom with its diversity of multilingual students. "But careful and detailed planning is the key to teaching non-English speaking children, that also need to learn about a new culture and a whole new way of life," she reiterates. This teacher's creativity and commitment permeate the entire program at University Park and set a standard of excellence and devotion for others in the building.

The Tile Wall of "International Images" University Park School, Denver, CO.

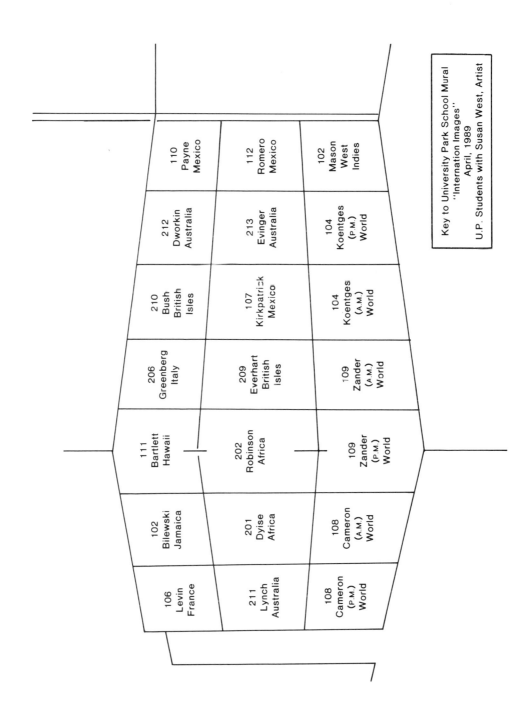

Key to University Park School Mural
"Internation Images"
April, 1989
U.P. Students with Susan West, Artist

110 Payne Mexico	212 Dworkin Australia	210 Bush British Isles	206 Greenberg Italy	111 Bartlett Hawaii	102 Bilewski Jamaica	106 Levin France
112 Romero Mexico	213 Evinger Australia	107 Kirkpatrick Mexico	209 Everhart British Isles	202 Robinson Africa	201 Dyise Africa	211 Lynch Australia
102 Mason West Indies	104 Koentges (P.M.) World	104 Koentges (A.M.) World	109 Zander (A.M.) World	109 Zander (P.M.) World	108 Cameron (A.M.) World	108 Cameron (P.M.) World

The Role of the Principal

We noted over and over in our descriptions of University Park's exciting programs how parent and family involvement stood out as a crucial factor. This parent participation could not occur without the planning, foresight and encouragement of University Park's outstanding principal, Dr. Karen Harvey. In her modest style, Dr. Harvey says that she and her staff want to respond to the needs of each child and that with such a rich cultural diversity, with so much for children and their families to give to others, the school cannot do other than utilize the resources that are present. During the past three years the school has welcomed families from: Nigeria, the Sudan, Japan, Korea, Malaysia, Jordan, Kuwait, Saudi Arabia, India, Chile, Italy, Turkey, Laos, Vietnam, Camodia, and other nations.

This principal attributes the extensive parental and community involvement in University Park programs to the fact that the school is always open and sincerely welcomes parents and other resource people. For example, University Park has its own "Publishing Center." Every first and second grader writes his or her own book during the school year. Parents come to assist in editing and printing the book on the school's computer, then it is illustrated and bound. The child's book is also stamped with the University Park Publishing Center stamp and each child receives a University Park bookmark to accompany the product. Through this school-wide project, alone, parents feel wanted and comfortable at University Park. "Some parents come only once," notes Dr. Harvey, "others come everyday. We have one father who comes to us on a regular basis, since he works at night; and another woman, who came one day to vote and enjoyed the school atmosphere so much, that now she comes to assist us three times a week, even though she has no children in the school."

What Can We Learn about Dealing with Difference?

What are the implications of University Park Primary School's programs for other elementary schools? Since we have emphasized in previous chapters that American schools' student populations everywhere today, are much like University Park's, what can we learn from this example? This school's successes demonstrate the value, for both students and teachers, of:

1. enlisting and encouraging parents, relatives, and other local community resource people, both multilingual and monolingual, to work in daily contact with the children.
2. identifying and utilizing adults who speak both the child's mother tongue and English for support, assessment and ongoing activities for non-English speaking children.
3. using strategies such as developing grant proposals for financial and matching support to fund long or short term projects in the school.
4. opening the school to the neighborhood and the community as a major source for identifying multiethnic, multilingual and crosscultural talent to stimulate and enrich the school's programs and the curriculum for a world perspective.

How Can Teachers Discover the Multiethnic Resources around Them?

If a teacher is to make the best use of the pluralism of the surrounding community, it is important to investigate the people and other resources that might contribute to the school's programs. Here are some suggestions that may prove pleasant diversions as well as stimulating fact-gathering experiences.

Start with Your Local Telephone Directory

Pick up the telephone directory in your city, town, or local area. First look through the white pages of the book for family names. Do you find listings of a number of Italian, Spanish, Greek, Chinese, Japanese, Arabic, or other identifiable ethnic family names? Does this tell you something about the ethnic makeup of your community? Also recall the names of schools, public parks, libraries or other public buildings in your city or town. Do the names of public buildings and schools give you some clues about the ethnic groups represented in your area?

Check the listing of restaurants in the yellow pages. You are likely to discover an interesting assortment of ethnic cuisines, and these restaurants are excellent multiethnic resources. Perhaps you could try a lunch or dinner at one of these establishments. Find out if any of the proprietors are parents in your school or live in the community. If they do, seek them out. These restauranteurs usually know a great deal about their ethnicity and background, since they are cooking and serving in the traditional ways of their culture. Often, ethnic restaurant proprietors and their families have chosen this means of livelihood because they wish to preserve aspects of their original culture now that they are in America. As a result, they may be willing to contribute to educational programs that promote the recognition and understanding of the variety of groups that make up multicultural America.

Another source to check in the yellow pages is listings of churches, synagogues, and more recently, mosques, funeral homes and private schools. All of these institutions can provide leads or information about the ethnic groups in your local community. Remember to refer to your school files as well to find out if officials in the ethnic organizations or business have children attending your school. These parents and families might be eager participants in school programs on ethnic heritage.

One final suggestion about telephone directories: it is a fascinating exercise to compare phone books of different cities. You gain new insights on the multiethnic composition of your own area when you compare and contrast it with other communities. Telephone directories for cities in the United States can be obtained for a minimal cost at your local telephone business office, or the local library or airport may have a variety of telephone directories you can use. Examine these telephone directories' white pages and yellow pages just as you did your own home-town directory. Make some hypotheses about the ethnic makeup of these other cities. Check your assumptions with friends or associates who have lived in or visited these cities. What similarities and differences did you find between the cities? What new understandings have you gained about your town or city as a result of these activities?

Look Up Government Documents

Another important source of data on the characteristics of various ethnic groups in the United States is the U.S. Census Bureau of the Department of Commerce, which publishes a wide range of documents and reports. Public libraries and university libraries contain special sections where the government documents are housed. The librarian or assistants can help you locate specific information from the documents, which are usually on microfiche with readers and copiers located conveniently at hand. For example, the U.S. Census Bureau puts out yearly reports with current population statistics and specialized reports on segments of that general population report. Some titles chosen at random are: "Data on the Spanish Ancestry Population Available from the 1980 Census of Population and Housing," or "Language Usage in the United States for 1985," or "Selected Characteristics of Person and Families of Mexican, Puerto Rican and Other Spanish Origins, 1986." Do not overlook this wealth of information that can help you put the ethnic groups in your community in a broader regional or national perspective. Watch for the most current U.S. Census Bureau reports, which will reflect the new waves of immigrants now coming from all parts of the globe.

Get Out into Your Community

Now that your interest about the ethnic composition of your area has been stimulated, the next step is to go out into the community and experience firsthand the variety of ethnic heritages existing there. Choose some ethnic restaurants that pique your interest and tastes. Have meals there. Try to speak with the owners. Ask them about their ties to their homelands or root cultures. Collect a number of menus. Find out who patronizes the ethnic restaurants. Particularly note if there are blends of American culture and the other culture represented. Describe these variations of customs and traditions and note your reactions to them. Your own attitudes are important for your later presentation of the ethnicity of the community to your students. It is essential that teachers understand their own attitudes toward the different groups of ethnics in their community because students are quick to sense both discomfort and easy acceptance.

Visit churches in your area. Talk to the clergy, ask about the languages and customs used during services. Observe the artifacts and ceremonial items used during the services and those that decorate both the inside and outside of the church, synagogue or mosque. Both the architecture and the art that adorns religious structures tell us much about the heritage and traditions of the members of that religion.

Social service organizations can also provide information about the ethnic characteristics of a community. Contact service organizations of different ethnic groups whose listings you have noted in the telephone directory. Interview the officials or directors of these agencies. Ask for their pamphlets, brochures or other literature. Ethnic business organizations can also be a source of information about the ethnic makeup of your community.

Plan for Exhibits, Displays and Programs with Ethnic Content

Most teachers are collectors by nature, and the local communty abounds in "cultural artifacts," everyday items that represent traditions, customs and folkways. It is interesting to call upon your local library and museums for resources and support in identifying the different groups in the area. Librarians in recent years have stressed the development of lists of ethnic books, both fiction and non-fiction, in their collections. Museums, particularly historical societies, have focused on exhibits and collections of local ethnic history and tradition and are excellent sources to tap both for background information and for use with students. Do not forget radio stations and the local television programs in your assessment of the ethnic resources in your community. Ethnic radio programs have become an important source of pride and ethnic interest in many communities in the past several years. Also watch for listings of ethnic movies in your community—not merely foreign-language films, but films that center on ethnic themes or describe the experiences of immigrants to the United States. Try to attend some ethnic movies, listen to a few ethnic radio broadcasts, and view some ethnic television programs. All of these activities will give you a better sense of the ethnic makeup of your community and the resources it has to offer.

Translating Ethnic Awareness to Your Classroom

Now that you have heightened your own awareness of the community in which you teach, you must consider ways of passing this sensitivity on to your students through the curriculum. In many instances, this can simply be a matter of retracing your initial investigations along with your class.

Analyze Your Own Reactions and Attitudes

Analyze your own reactions and attitudes toward the various ethnic groups you encountered during your investigation of the community. If particular ethnic practices and customs startled you when you first experienced them, consider this situation when you suggest similar experiences for the children in your classroom. For example, a visit to an ethnic restaurant, or social service organization will require tact and careful planning on the part of all parties involved—teacher, students and the ethnic hosts. Using the ethnic resources of the school community can be more complex and fraught with social implications than traditional field trips to the local fire station or the zoo, but the rewards can be much greater and much more far-reaching for you and your students.

As you encourage students to explore the ethnicity of their school community, encourage them to collect "cultural artifacts"—free and inexpensive materials that are representative of heritage and traditions. Next, prepare displays of these materials, discussing the artifacts in your classroom and then with other students, teachers and possibly parents.

Plan and Present Programs

Plan and present programs, exhibits, plays, meetings, cultural fairs and other types of group presentations to promote the multiethnic awareness of the community and the pride this brings to the locale.

If you are working with upper elementary school level children then using the local telephone directory to discover the ethnic makeup of the community is an exciting way to begin. Experiences in the use of the telephone directory are instructive activities for ten- eleven- and twelve-year-olds. Finding out what ethnic groups exist in the community, making plans for field trips and carrying out these plans are highly worthwhile learning experiences that involve many areas of the elementary school curriculum—reading, language arts, social studies, even mathematics and science. Art and music, dramatics and physical education could also conceivably be tied into these experiences.

Use a variety of media to extend your outreach into the multiethnic resources of your community. Consider appropriate television programs, films, filmstrips, videotapes, slides and slide/tape programs for the children's use. Does your local library or historical society have media materials featuring information and stories about various ethnic groups in the area?

You might be surprised at how many new resources have recently become available as a result of the continuing interest in ethnicity in the United States. Be sure to look for media materials that stress ethnic and cultural groups in the United States. While films about a typical family in Tokyo, a fisherman on a remote Italian island or the herders of a little-known African tribe can be interesting and educational, traditional world culture studies can easily overshadow the new goals of multicultural education. Elementary and secondary social studies have included the geography and history of other countries for decades. Aside from noting the role of immigrants in the Unites States, American education has only recently begun to recognize the variety of ethnic heritages that constitute American society and to include such studies in the curriculum.

Search for opportunities to combine media presentations with hands-on artifacts and collections or guest speakers and resource people. Children can obtain background information for learning more about specific ethnic groups through a film, videotape, television program or filmstrip. Then by examining the folk art or products, sampling foods unique to an ethnic tradition or meeting and speaking with a person who represents that ethnic heritage, new awareness and open attitudes are developed. Some of the recently published activity and lesson planning books and manuals for elementary school teachers contain activities in ethnic heritage.

View Multiethnic and Non-Sexist Education as Reaching into all Aspects of the Curriculum

Multiethnic education goes on throughout the school year and not just during a specified week or month (the traditional "Brotherhood" month, now renamed in many school districts because of its sexist overtones). This brings us to the additional awareness of non-sexist education, too. Dealing with differences and recognizing the ever-present dimension of the multiculturalism in our society, also sensitizes educators to the need for non-sexist, gender-neutral attitudes in teaching. If you feel the commitment to multiethnic, non-sexist education as an essential element in working with children, opportunities to incorporate these values into every subject of the curriculum, into the language arts and especially into the teaching of writing, into science, mathematics, music and art, as well as the social studies, will be ever present and available to you. Today, teaching with a multiethnic, non-sexist and worldminded view is an imperative!

Assessing Multiethnic Resources: A Questionnaire for Parents

Most elementary schools routinely send notes, announcements and flyers home to parents through the children, who bring replies back to class and to their teachers. So a questionnaire for parents and other relatives regarding ethnic activities is a familiar format for teachers to use to find out about resources that will enhance a program in multiethnic education. Additionally, it is possible that exciting new approaches to non-sexist, gender-free education will also arise through the responses to these questionnaires. You may discover women or men in non-traditional occupations and roles that provide wider options and role models for the children.

The example in the following questionnaire offers one possible format for your inquiry, but it can easily be modified to suit the specific situation.

Distribute the Ethnic Resources Questionnaire for Parents in the same manner you distribute other announcements and messages to parents. Explain to the children the contents and use of the questionnaire and the importance of its being returned to you so the results can be used in plans to enrich and augment the activities in the classroom. If the children encourage their parents to complete your questionnaire, you will surely receive a significant percent of response.

An Ethnic Resources Questionnaire for Parents

For Parents of Our Class
HELP US FIND OUT ABOUT OUR ETHNIC HERITAGE

Dear Parents:

Did you realize that there are many ways you can provide valuable resources to your child's education, to the classroom and the school? We are trying to find out about the ethnic heritage and background of the children in our class. We want to use this information about customs, traditions and heritage in our daily learning experience. Listed below are some ways you can make contributions to our educational programs. Please put a check mark beside the items that particularly interest you. Feel free to check as many items as you can. Then return this questionnaire with your child as soon as possible.

Thank you,

_____ Signed

☐ 1. I would like to volunteer with some activity in the classroom. ☐ Once a month
☐ Every two weeks ☐ On occasion

☐ 2. I have a car available for a field trip.

☐ 3. I would like to be on the "call list" for classroom helpers.

☐ 4. I have a talent related to my heritage and tradition I would like to share with the children; e.g., baking traditional bread or cookies, etc.

☐ 5. I have photos or slides related to an ethnic group the children might enjoy viewing. I would be glad to show them.

☐ 6. I have an educational program on my ethnic group I would like to present. It is

_____ .

☐ 7. I would like to help with an ethnic area project such as folk art or crafts.

☐ 8. I enjoy contributing ethnic food items when needed for class parties or programs.

☐ 9. I am musical and would like to share the music of my ethnic group with the children, e.g., playing an instrument, helping to teach a song.

☐ 10. I enjoy acting and would like to help prepare a play or skit related to my ethnic/gender background with the children.

☐ 11. I have an interesting business related to my ethnic/gender background the children might enjoy visiting. It is _____ . We can handle _____ children at one time.

☐ 12. The best time to reach me by telephone is: AM_____ PM_____ .

Child's Name _____ Our School _____

Parent's Name _____ Our Teacher _____

Address _____ Class _____

Telephone Number _____

Developing an Exchange Project with Other Schools

Using the pluralism of your local community can be an exciting technique to stimulate your daily classroom plans as well as long-range programs. But it can also be a springboard to broader ranging projects. Many teachers begin with ethnic awareness programs in their classrooms, then progress to ethnic exchange projects with other schools, either in the same locale or in distant states and regions of the United States or even Canada and Mexico. How do these ethnic group exchange projects between schools occur? How can teachers initiate and develop such exchange programs? What are the benefits derived from an exchange project with an ethnically different school?

Setting out Plans for an Ethnic Group School Exchange Program

For years teachers have been initiating and carrying out exchange programs with schools or specific classes in foreign countries. In the same way, exchange programs, usually through letter writing, drawing pictures or making slide/tape programs, can be developed between American schools of widely differing ethnic and racial affiliations. The first step is for the initiating elementary school to identify and trace its own members' ethnic backgrounds, using the activities and experiences suggested in this book. It is particularly helpful if the class compiles a scrapbook or diary combining the results of their research and investigations or develops a slide/tape show or photograph album portraying the ethnicities represented in the class.

Next, the children decide which ethnicity or heritage best represents the significant portion of the class. Perhaps there are several Greek Americans or Polish Americans; maybe a number of children have Native American or Hispanic ancestry. An ethnic heritage exchange project must focus on one or at most two dominant ethnicities or the ethnic theme of the project may become obscured.

The initiating school needs to consider how it will locate a school with which to hold the exchange. Among the teachers we worked with on inter-ethnic exchanges, one teacher knew of a school in another state that had a predominantly Arab-American student population. She felt this contact would be exciting and broadening for her students of mainly Anglo-American backgrounds. In another situation, the principal of a predominantly Hispanic school in the Southwest began an exchange with a school in the Southeastern region of the country, with children of mainly Appalachian or "old" English heritage. The first principal had developed his contacts with this school through a school administrators' conference where he met the other principal. Perhaps other school staff members or parents will provide contacts with an ethnically differing school so an ethnic exchange project can be initiated.

Once the initiating school has explored its own ethnic heritage and feels ready to present this information to the exchange school, then the exchange school or specific classroom groups in that school should be encouraged to send information, (possibly through computer networks if these are in place) visuals such as videotapes, letters, photos, drawings, etc. about its ethnic affiliations and traditions. The initiating school, in turn, reads and studies this material. For example, in the exchange between the Anglo-American classes and the school where Arab-American heritage predominated, the teacher engaged her students in:

1. locating and reading Arabic folk tales and literature;
2. listening to Arabic music;
3. exploring Middle Eastern art and architecture;
4. examining and critiquing books on the Middle East;
5. collecting current events information about this ethnic group;
6. collecting Middle Eastern/Arabic recipes;
7. hosting guest speakers of Middle Eastern/Arabic descent.

Stimulating the Exchange School

As the initiating school finds out about the ethnicity and heritage of the exchange school, so, in turn, the exchange school explores the ethnic resources of the initiating elementary school by:

1. reading and sharing the booklets, drawings, photos, albums, and other material prepared by the initiating school;
2. hearing guest speakers who are familiar with the ethnic resources of the initiating area (if these can be identified);
3. if upper level elementary school children are involved, reading articles and other information, (such as the local telephone directory or the computer network messages) describing the ethnic backgrounds of the initiating school's community.

Further activities between the two school groups may include:

1. choosing pen pals to exchange further communications, including interests, hobbies, favorite foods or descriptions of family and pets;
2. developing a slide/tape presentation or videotape to personalize the exchange of information between the two schools;
3. exchanging audio or video tapes that contain ethnic songs or instrumental music, classroom discussions and questions;
4. exchanging photographs of special occasions of ethnic significance in the community or festivals and ceremonies.

Culminating Activities

If the exchange school is a long distance from the initiating school, a visit will not be possible, but teachers can plan culminating activities such as a luncheon, program or fair featuring the traditions, foods, arts and crafts, music and customs of the ethnic groups represented in the exchange. Both groups should carry out these activities simultaneously at each of the schools. However, if it is practical to visit the exchange school, plan a visit tht involves a lunch with ethnic foods, traditions, customs and music for students, teachers and parents or a late afternoon or evening fair or program. Locate a video camera and videotape the event for the school's records and continued enjoyment. This sort of exchange program is the first step toward preparing children to live in a multiethnic society and multicultural world.

Tips for Teaching: So Close at Hand—Additional Ethnic Resources in Your Community

An enterprising educational supplier recently put out a limited number of posters, two in the set titled, "Talk to your Grandmother" and "Talk to Your Grandfather," for schools in the district where the firm was located. Featuring handsome portraits of a mature man and a mature woman, these posters for the elementary classroom were stunning reminders of one of our richest sources of ethnic heritage.

Our senior citizens—older aunts and uncles as well as grandparents and great-grandparents—can provide first-hand, stimulating accounts of settling and expansion of the locale or region. Most grandparents enjoy coming to the elementary school and speaking to the children about their experiences as immigrants to the United States or as settlers of the particular region. They often know a good deal about the local community, the landmarks, the buildings and the changes that have occurred over the years. Elders provide children with a link to the past and help youngsters gain a sense of tradition and belonging to their area.

Encourage the students in your class to contact their grandparents, great-grandparents or elder aunts and uncles. Consider using the same questionnaires (with modifications) presented earlier in this chapter to tap the resources of grandparents as well as parents to enrich multiethnic education in your school.

In addition to parents and relatives, other adults in the community can serve as resources for ethnic studies. Consider developing a variation of the Ethnic Resources Questionnaire for Parents to distribute among adults in the community who might not necessarily have children in your school but who might be willing to contribute their time, knowledge and energies to enhancing understanding of their heritage. (Recall the voter at University Park School, who was so impressed with the school when she came to vote that she returned to work in the school. If your school is a site for voters, take advantage of these occasions to tap ethnic resources.) Another area of resources is the local legislators or political figures, who may have experienced and overcome difficulties in their own education, going on to become polished speakers (frequently bilingual) and ethnically sensitive individuals.

Promoting the local color, facilities and interesting features of an area is one of the jobs of your local tourist bureau. If your community does not have such a service, then visit the local bus depot or train station, or airport for brochures, maps, posters or other materials that highlight the tradition and heritage of your community. You may be surprised to find out that city or town officials, or perhaps the local newspaper, have made a point of publicizing some unique traditions in your region. Find information about this heritage to pass on to your students or encourage them to uncover the information for themselves.

You may want to develop your own publication about your community's heritage and traditions, highlighting the ethnic groups that predominate in the area. For example, after a visit to the Littleton (Colorado) Historical Society, one early elementary teacher, currently on leave to work on her doctorate, realized the need for a guide to the Museum at the elementary school level. By working with the director and staff of the Littleton Historical Museum, the curriculum specialist and publications staff of the Littleton School district, second grade teachers and children, Janice Luellan, the author of *Our Little Town: The Littleton Community Grows Up!* (Littleton Public Schools, 1988) researched, wrote and developed a publication for the school district and a model for others in the Denver metropolitan area. Luellan's concern for multiethnic and non-sexist education and her desire to make Littleton and Colorado heritage come alive for its youngest citizens gave her the impetus to create this teacher's guide with accompanying student booklet. The Teacher's Guide includes lists of community resources, school district resources including books, films, videos, film strips; the facilities and programs offered by the Historical Museum, and classroom and "spin-off" activities for young children.

Do not overlook periodicals, usually monthly magazines, that feature the heritage and history of the state, city or region. Among the better known regional publications are *Arizona Highways* and *The New Mexican,* which abound with stunning photographs of the American Southwest's natural beauty and the fabulous folk art, crafts and ceremonies of the Indian tribes of the region. You may even come across children's story books or picture books about the region or locale. Be sure to ask your school librarian to check the Books in Print Catalog for such information, then obtain these children's books for your classroom. If no such children's books exist about tradition and heritage of your area, consider writing your own.

Summary

Ethnic scholars, such as Professor Ricardo Garcia, author of numerous books and articles on multilingual education, have reiterated the essence of our presentation in this chapter. When Garcia writes that our best teaching resources for multiethnic and multilingual education are within our communities, he reaffirms that a study of the local community would go far to explain the personal sacrifices and hardships its people have endured and the accomplishments they have made. All around us lie resources for multiethnic education. If teachers are committed to preparing children to live in a pluralistic world then the resources for this education are just inside and outside the schoolroom door.

References

Cuzzort, R. P. and King, E. W. *20th Century Social Thought,* 4th edition. Ft. Worth: Holt, Rinehart and Winston, 1989.

Denver Public Schools. Newsletter, Denver, Colorado: 1989.

Garcia, Ricardo. *Teaching in a Pluralistic Society.* second edition, N.Y.: Harper and Row, in press.

Luellan, Janice. *Our Little Town: The Littleton Community Grows Up!* Littleton, Colorado: Littleton School District, 1988.

Mead, Margaret. *Culture and Commitment.* Garden City: Doubleday, 1970.

5

The Teacher of Young Children as Researcher in Multicultural Settings

As we have emphasized in the preceding chapter, teachers of young children must recognize that currently and for the future, they will be teaching children from widely varying ethnic, racial and social backgrounds—a far cry from those majority Anglo pupils found in most schools in past decades. These multiethnic and multilingual school populations present new challenges and new opportunities for teachers that perhaps were not addressed in their teacher education programs and professional training. Because of the changing climate in elementary school classrooms of ethnically diverse children, this educational sociologist designed an investigation into the dynamics of teacher and pupil interactions in multilingual/multicultural early childhood settings.

Promising Practices in Teaching Ethnically Diverse Young Children

In Denver, Colorado, as in many cities and towns, new immigrant populations have drastically changed the enrollments from majority white middle class students. Denver has been the host to a wide range of new immigrant groups from all parts of the globe, but the numbers of Hmong from Southeast Asia, newly arrived Mexicans from across the border, and Vietnamese of the "boat people" migration have stood out as larger groups of widely differing students in Denver public schools. Elementary schools with concentrations of these and other non-English speaking young children were the sites for the research project "Identifying Promising Practices in Teaching Ethnically Diverse Children in the Elementary School." Funded by the Western Interstate Consortium on Higher Education (WICHE), the Denver Public Schools and the University of Denver, the investigation was designed and carried out by me and my graduate research assistants, who were also early childhood teachers on leave from the Denver schools.

The selection of classrooms with ethnically diverse children, aged four to eight years—early childhood education to second grade—from seven different Denver public schools was the initial step in the research. This choice of age level was made because of the organization of Denver elementary schools. Further, extensive literature in the field of child growth and development indicates that the early years of schooling are crucial in the child's intellectual and social development.

As the director of the project, I made an initial visit to each of the schools in the study. After interviewing the principal at each school, a schedule of visitations for the research team was organized. A total of 53 classrooms and 53 different early elementary school teachers was identified for the study. The researchers were able to actually observe and therefore include in this study a total of 32 classrooms with their teachers.

The three instruments developed for use in observing and interviewing the classroom teachers involved in the study were:

- The Multicultural Classroom Checklist for Identifying Promising Practices in Ethnically Diverse Classroom;
- The Teacher Assessment of Non-English Speaking Children's Achievement and Progress;
- An Interview with Teachers of Ethnically Diverse Children.

Each ethnically diverse classroom in the study was observed for one full morning or one full afternoon session. The observers used the "Multicultural Classroom Checklist" which assessed the broad areas of 1) classroom environment, including a diagram of the physical arrangements, descriptions of bulletin boards, texts and materials used; 2) social interactions in the classroom; 3) rules and routines of the classroom; 4) cultural continuity in the classroom; 5) innovative strategies used by the teacher for working with ethnically diverse children.

Each teacher was personally interviewed to inquire about such activities as working with parents, personal background, education, travel, and general attitudes about the ethnically diverse class. Each teacher was asked to fill out an assessment of the non-English speaking children's achievement and progress in his or her classroom. The results from the data gathered with these three instruments were then tabulated.

The results revealed through the ratings of individual teachers on the "Multicultural Classroom Checklist," present a profile of the type of teacher who is effectively functioning with ethnically diverse pupils in general terms. This is a teacher who creates the sense that school is a good place to be; and an atmosphere of warmth and stimulation for active learning. This teacher individualizes the entire curriculum for each child, interacting some time during each day in a positive and supportive manner with each child in the class. There are many alternatives to choose from for fulfilling the daily academic work. For example, children might learn the vowel sounds during their music time through singing the vowels.

Much praise and encouragement characterize this teaching style. There is never any scolding, yelling or deprecation of children. Children in this classroom are relaxed and unrestricted in their movements about the room. The classroom reflects the ethnic heritage and background of all the children in the group. Newspaper clippings and articles about Hispanic, Hmong, Vietnamese, Arabic or other ethnic groups are found on bulletin boards. Artifacts such as weavings, sculptures, painting, photographs and folk art adorn the tables, desks and border of the room, reflecting the varieties of heritages the children represent. The teacher refers to these aspects of the material culture of the children during the daily learning activities and this material remains displayed throughout the school year—not just appearing for special occasions only to be replaced by the symbols of solely the majority Anglo culture.

This model for the teacher of ethnically diverse children is deeply concerned about contacts with the families of the children. The teacher makes efforts to learn a few words of the language the children speak, and to learn about the religious backgrounds, customs, traditions, holidays, festivals and practices of the children. This model teacher will then incorporate this information into the daily learning experiences of the children.

The classrooms of these model teachers reveal a physical arrangement where children work together, face to face, in small or larger groups. The rooms are organized to allow many alternatives for children, easily accessible to the children themselves with minimum teacher supervision. Children are not stereotyped by either their ethnic or racial identity or by their academic ability. *No progress charts publicly announce a child's progress or the lack of it.*

Finally, these teachers show their respect for the children they teach by involving them in planning for daily activities as well as special occasions. Children in these classrooms, from four-year-olds to eight-year-olds, have responsibilities for setting out and putting away materials, organizing their free time activities, keeping the classroom tidy, greeting visitors, decorating the room and so on.

Some Specific Promising Practices

Several classroom settings revealed uniquely creative and innovative techniques for teaching ethnically diverse children. These include:

1. At the Early Childhood and Kindergarten Levels—In the classrooms of several kindergarten and early childhood programs, teachers had utilized the classrooms' location in the school buildings and the special entrances into the classroom that had been provided. When parents and family members came to pick up their children, these teachers initiated conversations to make contact with the parents and promote family involvement. Especially for parents of non-English speaking children, usually people who were new arrivals to the United States, this strategy afforded an informal and comfortable access to the school, to their child's classroom and to conversations with their child's teacher. Hence, these early childhood teachers had obtained in-depth knowledge of their pupils, their families, their needs and their aspirations for the children as a result of the contacts.

2. At the First Grade Level—In the classroom of one First Grade teacher observed during the study, a unique system of "buddies" had been developed. The teacher had paired Anglo children with various new immigrant children, Southeast Asian, Mexican, or Arabic, for reading and language arts activities, for mathematics and for simple science experiences. The children communicated well, each pair contributing to the activity and the learning experience. The teacher had carefully worked on creating an atmosphere of mutuality, of interchange and equal status for the partners so that the Anglo children did not dominate or feel superior to their non-Anglo "buddies." This buddy system appeared to be helping limited or non-English speaking children learn English more quickly and easily, as well.

3. At the Second Grade Level—Another promising practice for initial orientation of ethnically diverse children was developed by a Second Grade teacher. This was a series of slide-tape shows consisting of an introduction to the school building, its personnel and its facilities. (This technique could also be accomplished with a videotape.) The slide show had one "standard" set of slides with accompanying audiotapes in five different languages—the languages of the new ethnic groups now enrolling their children in this school. The slide-tape show helped to ease the entry to this multicultural school for both child and parent.

Promising practices for working with ethnically diverse young children in elementary school classrooms reveal how crucial the nature of the classroom organization is in itself. An organization that fosters individualizing, providing many alternatives, and stimulating active learning approaches is the MOST EFFECTIVE strategy for teaching ethnically diverse children—and for teaching ALL children.

Studies in Britain on the Teaching of Mother Tongue

Another nation that has great interest and much concern for the teaching of English to non-English speaking children is Britain. A number of projects have been carried out at universities located in cities with identifiable, multiethnic, non-English speaking populations such as London, Birmingham and Bradford. We will describe several of these projects particularly focusing on ethnically diverse groups of young children.

The Linguistic Minorities Project, University of London

The Linguistic Minorities Project, funded by the British Department of Education and Science for three years was based at the Institute of Education, University of London. The overall aim of the Linguistic Minorities Project was to recognize and analyze the many patterns of bilingualism that exist in multicultural Britain. The staff of the Project was a multidisciplinary team that was charged with assessing the current methods of teaching English language to non-English speaking pupils in both the normal (public) schools and in the classes organized by the minority groups themselves. The team also had responsibility for developing a sociolinguistic survey and a more detailed study of patterns of language use and attitudes toward language. The Project charted languages from southern and eastern Europe and south and east Asia that were in use in various cities and towns across Britian. The Linguistic Minorities Project research resulted in findings that had a bearing on a wide range of both theoretical and practical issues in the field of sociolinguistics and education.

Among these findings were that parents of recently immigrated groups are very concerned with the maintenance of the mother tongue to facilitate communication with their children, the children's ability to participate and communicate in family gatherings, and ensuring contact with the homeland. Further these parents are often worried about their children's loss of self esteem and identification with their family culture and religion. On the other hand, most British teachers are pre-occupied with the social, psychological and general educational performance of their pupils. It is interesting to note that in Britian there is no accepted concept of "hyphenated identities"—Italian-American, Mexican-American, Polish-American—as there is in America. Further, few minority languages are valued or publicly recognized in the wider British society.

The researchers of the Linguistic Minorities Project, as they worked with and studied children, noted that many children actually stopped speaking their mother tongues and at times, even refused to acknowledge the existence of their other languages. These experts felt that it was an indication that young children realized the relative value accorded to English versus their mother tongues, both at school and in the wider society. In some cases minority children refused to speak the mother tongue at home except when essential, for example, with a non-English-speaking parent. This could cause the loss of total communication between parents and children in some minority families even before the child starts school.

The Children's Language Project

Traditionally in American schools, children speaking a language other than English were seen as struggling against an impediment that needed to be eradicated before they could successfully acquire the English language and thus take advantage of the learning opportunities available. But in more recent years since the waves of non-English speaking children have entered American classrooms, a shift in thinking has been underway. Now instead of regarding the mother tongue as a barrier to learning English, more educators and classroom teachers are coming to see it as providing children with a valuable foundation of confidence at using language and understanding of how language works. Language and culture are inseparable as teachers have discovered through their efforts to incorporate aspects of their pupils' home cultures into the day to day work of the classroom. Gradually, then they are recognizing that the multicultural curriculum should also be a multilingual one; and the development of relevant classroom strategies and curriculum materials is becoming a major priority to meet the needs of ethnically diverse school populations.

As we have noted, British schools have been dealing with large numbers of non-English speaking immigrants. In response to the needs for curriculum materials and teaching methods to deal effectively with ethnically and linguistically diverse groups of children, research and development projects have been initiated. One of the most notable of these projects was the Children's Language Project which brought together some of the most highly regarded linguistic experts and creative British primary school educators in the country. The Children's Language Project was designed with the ultimate aim of responding to the growing interest of all primary teachers in the diversity of language experiences that children bring into school, by providing them with resouces for classroom activities. The Children's Language Project set out to give teachers a series of starting points from which to encourage their pupils to explore and appreciate their own linguistic repertoires as well as linguistic diversity around them. The materials the Project developed were intended to help teachers integrate the out-of-school language experiences of the children with the language demands of the classroom; to develop both their own and their pupils' awareness of different languages and variety of language, and the circumstances in which they are used. Further, it drew upon the language resources of all members of the school community, including non-teaching staff, families and local people.

Another important concern of the Children's Language Project was to prompt teachers to examine their expectations when planning and evaluating work in the classroom and the school, particularly with regard to the use of different regional or social varieties of English or languages other than English. And it raised questions about what the languages and dialects people speak may mean for different ethnic and social groups, as well as their awareness of the relation between language use and cultural traditions and values. In other words, the social class implications of language use.

The Children's Language Project materials are comprised of a pack of four student activity cards. These activity cards are like posters with double-sided panels that measure $8 \times 11\frac{1}{2}$ inches in size. Each student activity card focuses on a particular theme relating to some aspect of children's experience of language. The themes for the four "cards" are: Languages at Home; Languages at School; Languages Around Us; Languages Near and Far. There is an accompanying teachers' guide that offers guidance on the rationale underlying the student activity cards; ways of extending the activities; a list of local resources such as libraries and bookstores, publishers, associations, translation units, and a bibliography. The teachers' guide also features the writing, illustrations and photographs done by children during the developmental and piloting stages of the curriculum materials project.

The activity cards were planned with the 7–11 age group in mind. However, these materials have been adapted and used with younger children and highschoolers, as well. Although the activity cards work best in classrooms where students work cooperatively in small groups (the British Primary Method) the cards can be used by individual children or with a whole class. The cards also encourage the participation of parents and other members of the family, and of local resource people. The Children's Language Project staff designed the materials with a lot of flexibility so that the classroom teacher can decide which card is best to use and in what sequence and how best to introduce the material to the children. When assessing the results of the uses of the Children's Language Project, the developers found that teachers reported the material was more effective if it was used over a period of time, rather than as a one-time activity. Ideally, teachers reported, the advantages of the material came from the multilingual dimension it provided that might otherwise be difficult to incorporate in traditional language learning programs. This leads us to examining a specific example of non-English speaking children in the British primary school.

A British Case Study of Two Immigrant Boys

Now we turn to the investigations of Daphne Brown, a head mistress and teacher who worked for over twenty years in five different primary schools with multicultural populations. In her book, *Mother Tongue to English: The Young Child in the Multicultural School,* she details a case study of two young Bangladeshi brothers, Saba, age six and a half, and Asad, age five and a half, who spoke only Bengali when they arrived to be enrolled by their parents at the assigned primary school.

Daphne Brown observed the two boys in two different classrooms daily for three months. She classified each verbal expression under differing headings including: expressions using Bengali, expressions using English, remarks of other children about the brothers, remarks made by adults to or about the boys, physical contacts between the boys and children, between the boys and adults. The results of the observations were categorized into four groups: use of mother tongue, Bengali, use of the English language; aspects of second language development; and the physical aspects. The conclusions in this research brought out some pertinent and meaningful results for those who work with ethnically diverse young children.

1) the five-year-old Bengali speaking boy had more advantages being in the entry class, than his six-year-old brother in the class with children, just one year older. This was due to the fact that there are more explanations and directions to be presented in the instruction of the six-year-olds than with the "fives."

2) It was necessary and even essential for the teacher in the "reception class" to give time for educating children in general basic behavior at school, such as how to use the toilet, how to care for equipment, how to line up to receive milk or to go out to the playground. The younger boy (Asad) benefitted from the teacher's detailed instructions while the older boy (Saba) had to watch the other children continually and try to copy their behavior, since the "sixes" were now expected to know just what to do during these routine activities.

3) The pace in the beginning class (as in the kindergartens in the United States) was slower in that there was more time for cleaning up after activities, lining up, dressing in the cloakroom, etc. The older children were more independent and could do these activities faster, leaving Saba less time to figure out what was going on and what he had to do.

4) The relationship between the teacher and the children in the younger boy's classroom was more demonstrative—facial expressions, the tone of voice and the movement of hands, the assistance given to the children when dressing or putting on painting aprons with reassuring hand clasps, were far more prevalent with the adults and children in the "reception" class than they were in the older children's class.

5) Asad, and also many of the other children in the reception class, devoted a considerable proportion of their time to parallel play when there was no need or desire to communicate verbally with any other child. This lack of involvement in cooperative play eased the pressure which is imposed upon a non-English speaking child during situations involving a considerable amount of language. Saba was frequently caught up in the natural group activities of the older children and they often proved very demanding for both him and the children with whom he was trying to play and converse.

6) Asad's egocentric speech increased as he became more confident, and relaxed in his own activities, and gradually English words were introduced into his Bengali repertoire—these were repeated and so were the new English phonemes. Thus, uninhibited he was helping himself to master new sounds. Saba was never heard repeating English words to himself.

7) In the reception class there appeared to be more situations in which Asad could succeed or even excel among the five-year-olds, activities such as buttoning, or distributing milk. Saba, however, found difficulty in competing with the capabilities of those in his class, where there were more situations that demanded a command of English.

In summing up her position on the non-English speaking child, Daphne Brown writes with the typical English directness and eloquence:

> A child who cannot speak English is not a dumb child; he had within himself the heritage of a rich expressive language belonging to his own culture. This language is not just a string of words which automatically becomes obsolete as he ventures across the threshold of the school, it is part of his very being which has developed within him since the first moment when his mother cradled him in her arms and shared with him her own form of speech. Through his mother tongue the child has learned to communicate, to express his feelings, to reason, to question and to discover—should any teacher bypass such an integral part of his life, unheeding his words simply because she has neither the time nor the understanding to comprehend their message? It is essential that the immigrant or ESL child should be able to express his feelings verbally within the classroom from the first moments he enters school even though his words may not be understood by anyone else. (Daphne Brown, 1979, p. 26)

These British investigations of non-English speaking young children bring new insights to our understandings of working with ethnically diverse students and their families in our schools.

A Multiethnic Study of Young Children in Australia

Another nation that has developed a growing awareness of its multiculturalism is Australia. We now consider a research study that involved widely diverse young children in Australian kindergartens. After a number of years specializing in the teaching, research and administration of early childhood education in the United States, Dr. Margery Camaren moved to Western Australia to continue her work in crosscultural dimensions in higher education there. The following material is adapted from the research in multicultural early childhood education she did while in residence as an educator in Western Australia.

The purpose of this study was to test the universality of the relationship of attractiveness and valued social attributes among ethnic groups in a multiethnic environment. The study took place in Perth, Western Australia, using three groups of kindergartners—girls only — representing the dominant (Anglo), ethnic minority (Italian), and visible minority (Aboriginal) sub-cultures of the geographic area.

This study is particularly pertinent to present-day Australia which has its traditions and values embedded in British culture. The geographical isolation of Western Australia, combined with its small population concentrated in Perth, the capital city, make the British orientations even more pronounced, so that a frequent comment is that the area is "more English than England." As such, Anglo dominance is strongly reflected in the values of the community as expressed in the media and the daily way of life. Yet, the Anglo value system is in sharp contrast to the ethnic make-up of the population in which fewer than 40% of the residents are native-born Australians. The population of Western Australia reflects a migration policy which encouraged predominantly Anglos until the 1960s, when other groups, such as Southern Europeans and East Asians, began to arrive. The native Australians, the Aboriginals, constitute only a small number of the total Australian population but are a highly visible ethnic group in the metropolitan area of Perth. Increased migration from non-English speaking countries and the growing awareness of the Aboriginals of their uniqueness has brought attention to multiculturalism in Australian society.

Dr. Camaren chose kindergartens as the focus of her multicultural research project. These kindergartens, operated by the Western Australian Education Department, were free government sponsored early childhood facilities with child populations representing diverse ethnic groups. From this multiethnic population a sample of 90 kindergarten girls was chosen, representative of the targeted ethnic groups—Anglo Australian, Italian Australian, Aboriginal. The children in the study were shown photographs mounted on poster board of little girls their own age, representing these three ethnic groups. (Standardization of the photos was carefully planned so that each child-photo was the same size and displayed only the child's face.) The kindergarten girls in the study were shown these photo boards and asked to indicate, by pointing to the appropriate photo, their responses to the following questions: Who is friendly to other children? Who says angry things? Is not afraid of anything? Might hurt you? Does not hit even if someone else hits first? Hits without good reason? Does not need help from anyone? Scares you? Does not like shouting? And lastly, Who do YOU think is pretty?

The results of this study confirm what early childhood educators have known for some time; that kindergartners (five-year-olds) of differing ethnic backgrounds were ethnically aware and able to pick out like-ethnic peers. In this research the findings indicated that Anglo Australian children's choices of "who was pretty" were more like adults' choices than were the choices of the Italian Australian or Aboriginal children. However, all groups chose the Anglo faces as attractive, marking the influence of the dominant culture on what is considered "pretty." Additionally, social attributes, ethnicity and attractiveness were closely linked. Anglo children's photos were selected by all three ethnic groups and accorded valued social attributes such as friendly, does not hit, etc.; and low antisocial attributes—says angry things; might hurt you, etc. On the other hand, Aboriginal children's photos were assigned low ratings for the valued social attributes and rated high on antisocial attributes—even by the Aboriginal children themselves!

From this study and others like it that have been conducted in recent years, there can be little doubt that young children have already developed attitudes about self and others based on ethnicity and appearance. Norms of physical attractiveness exist and are associated with valued social behaviors and antisocial behaviors in cultures everywhere. Young children are socialized with and then, internalize these opinions forming the basis for their attitudes and values. It is important for educators to realize that children may be growing up with the notion that if a person is blue-eyed, blond and beautiful; anything they do must be right, lovely, and acceptable. This investigation of the young children's perceptions of physical attractiveness and its relation to social behavior informs teachers of the needs to focus on far more than the academic aspects of the curriculum, such as language and mathematics, science and social studies. The social aspects of the classroom are as crucial as cognitive learning to self development and a successful life in a multicultural society.

Tips for Teachers as Classroom Researchers

Too often elementary school teachers are heard to say that they are so involved and immersed in their daily classroom activities, that they could not possibly have any time left over for such esoteric activities as classroom research. This is an erroneous and truly disappointing attitude on the part of teachers. Research in your classroom can go on as part of one's daily lesson plans and organization. Investigating the classroom climate for learning, the interactions of one's students, the impact of a particular topic, project, specific curriculum material, or intensive program can be exhilarating and very informative. The classroom teacher can build a component of research into the lesson plans for any activity or project—many times we term it "evaluation" and are doing research without even realizing it. Educational researchers at times assert that only the teachers involved in their research can interpret the relevance of the study for actual classroom practice, since teachers are the ones who are really knowledgeable about what goes on in their classrooms. The ideal situation is to encourage classroom teachers—especially in early childhood settings—to design and carry out research projects and investigations as teacher-researchers. In the example that follows we hope to encourage classrooms teachers to consider opportunities to develop research projects right in their classrooms.

A Crosscultural Experiement: *Teresa's Scrapbook*

How effective are multicultural curriculum materials developed in one dominant English-speaking multiethnic society and transported to another? This was a curriculum research project that we set out to implement. We introduced the series, SCRAPBOOKS, written by Gillian Klein and illustrated by Simon Wilby and Bridgett Hill (Methuen Children's Books, Inc. 1984) to an early childhood classroom in a school in the American Southwest. SCRAPBOOKS is a series of multicultural books for young children developed in Britain for children in all white areas, as well as for those in cosmopolitan areas where many ethnic minorities attend the schools. Each of the books in the SCRAPBOOK series features children from ethnic minority cultures who return for a visit to their country of origin, then come back to their school in Britain to share some of their experiences with their teacher and classmates, through the medium of their scrapbooks. The sharing of experiences of other cultures and traditions is at the heart of SCRAPBOOKS. The books bring the children's experiences and observations from abroad back into the classroom. The final frame of each book focuses on an activity in a specific area of the curriculum. The Teacher's Notes that accompany the books detail information and activities for follow-up after using the books with the children. This series of books for use with four, five, and six year-olds is designed to encourage and support language learning and concept development. The stunning pictures and the charming story lines enhance classroom discussions and motivate young children to participate in further projects suggested by the multiethnic themes of the books. Five countries are included in the SCRAPBOOK series, Trinidad, The Punjab in India, a village in Spain, Hong Kong, and Cyprus.

The American early childhood classroom of four and five year olds in which this curriculum research project took place was composed of mainly Spanish speaking children, whose families had recently immigrated from Mexico. The teacher chose the title, *Teresa's Scrapbook,* that highlighted Teresa's visit to Spain. The Spanish words in the story represented the mother tongue of many of the children in this eary childhood classroom and hence seemed most appropriate for this crosscultural study.

A day in early December was set for the initial activities of presenting the story to the class. I arrived at the school, notebook in hand, to observe the occasion. The class that day was composed of 15 five-year-olds, two mother-assistants, a Spanish speaking classroom teacher's aide and the head teacher, Dr. Marjorie Milan. Dr. Milan had prepared for this multicultural experience by reading the Teacher's Notes accompanying the SCRAP-BOOKS series, noting the remarks specifically prepared for "Teresa's Scrapbook," and supplementing this with material and an art project from her own file of resources. A beautiful artbook and photographs from Dr. Milan's visit to the Alhambra in Spain, seemed most appropriate to augment the presentation of "Teresa's Scrapbook." Further, a stimulating art project to design many-colored "tile" squares for decorating interiors fit well with the descriptions of the grand palace, the Alhambra, and its unique and "lovely patterns all over the inside," featured in the story of Teresa's vist to Granada and her tour of the Alhambra.

The activity began with the children arranging themselves on the floor by Dr. Milan, their teacher, in the usual story time setting. As she presented and read "Teresa's" story describing her visit to Espana and the Alhambra, Dr. Milan interspersed the account with photographs she had taken of the magnificent grounds of the Palace and pictures from the English edition of a color photographic study of the Alhambra's artwork and architectural significance. The children listened with rapt attention. When appropriate, their teacher used the Spanish words that appear in the vocabulary list at the end of "Teresa's Scrapbook." She translated each work, such as **la casa,** the house, **las montanas,** the mountains, **el palacio,** the palace, from English to Spanish and vice versa. The children could then hear both the Spanish and English terms being spoken in their learning environment.

When the story was concluded Dr. Milan passed around her photographs for the children to examine more closely, as well as the book, *Teresa's Scrapbook.* The mother-assistants and the teacher's aide also participated in viewing the pictures and discussing Teresa's story. Next, Dr. Milan suggested that it would be exciting to make "our own Alhambra interior" by creating many tile designs from different colored squares. She had a sample of several squares of tile designs already prepared to help the children visualize what their art project would look like. Then instructing her adult aides, she had them place three large chart-like sheets of white paper in several locations on the classroom floor. The children were divided into three groups, so that each group could gather around the chartpaper. The aides gave each child a packet of squares of varying colors and sizes.

The children went to work with enthusiasm and vigor creating numerous squares with interesting and individual designs and colors. Then they pasted their squares onto the chart paper, simulating the walls of the Palace. They appeared to be highly motivated and excited about this art activity. The children spoke to each other in both Spanish and English as they went about their tasks.

What were the outcomes of this crosscultural experiment and curriculum research design? When the class ended for the day, we discussed the outcomes of the crosscultural experience for the children, for the teacher and for the adult aides (mothers) in the group. The following conclusions were reached:

1. appropriate multiethnic curriculum materials can be transported from one culture to another successfully as demonstrated by this experiment in an early childhood classroom where a number of Spanish speaking children and adults easily related to a story describing Spanish tradition and using some Spanish language.

2. the story "Teresa's Scrapbook" presented the teacher with opportunities to develop an art project with the children, stimulated small muscle activities, enhanced their creative talents, and gave them information and knowledge about the cultural and artistic heritage of the world.

3. the activity provided opportunities for the mother assistants and the aide who are Spanish speaking to find reason for pride and identification with a heritage related to their own, in the classroom setting and in the school thereby providing important parent involvement.

4. the series of books, SCRAPBOOKS, stimulated the teacher to develop future classroom projects combining multicultural and multilingual experiences and cognitive learning experiences.

It was concluded that well conceived and creatively illustrated multicultural curriculum materials for young children can be successfully used in classrooms and schools in diverse cultures and many nations. Further, the highly experienced early childhood educator who directs the program where we implemented this curriculum research project is a staunch advocate of research for the classroom teacher. In this chapter we have presented accounts and descriptions of investigations in classrooms of ethnically diverse young children to demonstrate the feasibility of combining research while teaching, especially where social values such as attitudes towards race, class and gender are involved.

References

Brown, Daphne. *Mother Tongue to English: The Young Child in the Multicultural School*. London: Cambridge University Press, 1979.

Camaren, Margery. "The Influence of Ethnicity and Perceptions of Physical Attractiveness on Children's Attributions of Social Behavior". unpublished doctoral dissertation. School of Education. University of Denver. 1982.

Children's Language Project Team. *The Children's Language Project*. London: Institute of Education, University of London. 1984.

Goodman, Maryellen. *The Culture of Childhood*. New York: Teachers College Press. 1970.

Kahn, Verity. "The Mother-Tongues of Linguistic Minorities in Multicultural England." *Journal of Multilingual and Multicultural Development,* Vol 1. No. 1, 1980, pp. 71–88.

King, Edith. "Promising Practices in Teaching Ethnically Diverse Children" *Momentum:* Journal of the National Catholic Educational Association, Vol. 14, No. 1, (Feb, 1983), pp. 38–40.

Klein, Gillian and Willby, Simon. *SCRAPBOOKS*. London: Methuen Children's Books, 1984.

Woods, Peter. *Inside Schools: Ethnography in Educational Research*. London: Routledge and Kegan Paul, 1986.

6

Future Directions for Teaching Ethnic and Gender Awareness

How Has Heightened Awareness of Diversity Affected Teaching in the Elementary Schools?

In order to look forward to the future of multiethnic and non-sexist education, we must take stock of the past. Much change has occurred in the past two decades in these aspects of education. First known as Ethnic Heritage Studies or bicultural and bilingual education (educators were hardly aware of non-sexist education) this concept has quickly expanded to encompass multicultural education. Multicultural Education, as the title of a number of recent texts will attest, has become the umbrella term for dealing with diversity in a pluralistic society. This diversity is now being stretched to include teaching "special" children—physically handicapped, mentally retarded, emotionally disturbed, gifted and talented, and so on, as individual differences have been highlighted through research findings and the commitment to equal opportunity in education.

However, it was the Bicentennial Year celebrations in 1976 and the popularity of books like Alex Haley's ROOTS; Michael Novak's *The Rise of the Unmeltable Ethnics;* Irving Howe's *World of Our Fathers* and Bill Hosokawa's *The Quiet Americans* that helped transform ethnic heritage studies into multicultural studies. American educators, as part of the broader society became sensitized to the need for multicultural education. Most recently, the label "multicultural education" is the term being used by teachers, curriculum specialists and ethnic scholars, who have developed definitions such as the following:

> **Multicultural education** is at least three things, an idea or concept, an educational reform movement, and a process. **Multicultural education** incorporates the ideas that all students—regardless of their gender and social class, and their ethnic, racial or cultural characteristics—should have an equal opportunity to learn in school. Another important idea in multicultural education is that some students, because of these characteristics, have a better chance to learn in schools as they are currently structured than do students who belong to other groups or have different cultural characteristics. (J. A. Banks, 1989, p. 2)

James Lynch in his book on prejudice reduction in the schools, describes **multicultural education** as generally regarded as focusing on the special needs of minority group children, the need for a change in attitude and understanding in the majority and the needs of all pupils to feel creatively comfortable with cultural diversity as the norm. (Lynch, 1987, p. 7)

Multicultural education as defined by Sleeter and Grant in their book, *Making Choices for Multicultural Education,* is termed educational practices directed toward race, culture, language, social class, gender and handicap, although in selecting it they do not imply that race is the primary form of social inequality. Sleeter and Grant see racism, classism and sexism as equally important with handicappism having been created partly as a result of these three categories. (Sleeter and Grant, 1988, p. 26)

These ethnic scholars and noted educators call for multicultural education to encompass every aspect of the curriculum. Multicultural education should be incorporated into all subject areas from early childhood education to higher education. They urge that regard for pluralism and diversity be part of all school activities and projects. Further, they reiterate that multiculturalism and therefore, multicultural education is an international movement. It is found in nations across the globe and most particularly in developed countries that have seen large influxes of immigrants and refugees in recent decades, nations such as Britian, Canada, France, Germany, Australia, as well as the United States.

That a deep concern and commitment to non-sexist education is included in these conceptions of what is considered multicultural education is a new dimension for teachers and administrators to note. What is non-sexist, gender-neutral education? For teachers at the elementary school levels, it is having an awareness and hence, expressing in attitudes and actions that young girls and young boys are equal human beings. This then means that teachers do not stereotype children by their sex. Classroom activities, books and other curriculum materials, learning programs and evaluations should take place in an atmosphere of equality of opportunity for both boys and girls.

Influences and Trends

Recent research projects and publications, as well as the titles of national conferences, regional meetings and colloquia reveal a general shift from themes labeled "multiethnic"; "ethnic studies" and even "multicultural" to broader terminology such as "education for a diverse society" or as explicit as "sex stereotyping and education." These conferences and seminars now focus on examining and exploring the complexities of teaching in contemporary educational settings in which the forces of sexism, racism and classism are played out in multicultural and multilingual classrooms. Research projects sponsored by school districts, state education offices, universities, as well as, doctoral dissertation research, are designed to consider how these forces delineate institutional arrangements and cultural patterns which create inequalities in our society. So critical have some commentators on the educational scene become that they declare no educational policy, curriculum or program is ideologically or politically innocent, rather they are inextricably related to issues of social class, ethnicity, gender and power. (McLaren, 1989)

To pique your own sensitivity and awareness to the climate for pluralism and diversity in a school or a specific classroom, test yourself on the following questions by using your own school, classroom, or schools and classrooms with which you are familiar or have visited recently. How much detail and response can you give to observations about the concern for differing ethnic, racial, religious and social class groups in the school?

Ask Yourself, Have I Noticed:
1. What decorations—photographs, pictures, posters, banners, artifacts, trophies, murals, showcases and so on, in the halls and in the classrooms reflect the ethnic heritages of the children and families that attend and use the school? And do the offices of the school's administrators, social worker, speech therapist, school nurse or clinic reflect the ethnic heritages of the children? Does the lunchroom, cafeteria or area designated for eating meals, the multipurpose room, auditorium and gymnasium display the hallmarks and traditions of those who presently attend the school, as well as those who once attended it?

2. Are there evidences of the use of other languages than English? Signs in other languages? Writing in script of other languages? Oral uses over the intercom system, radio, or use of audiotapes, etc?

3. Did you note and examine some multicultural curriculum materials in the classrooms, such as textbooks, kits, filmstrips, artifacts, magazines? Describe them. What are their titles? Where were they published? When?

4. Does the organization of the school foster recognition of diverse ethnic groups? Are parents, aides, resource persons of differing ethnic, racial, and international backgrounds involved in teaching, in programs, projects and activities in and around the school?

5. Does the school staff model and reflect differing groups in the community or neighborhood or is the staff mainly mono-ethnic and mostly of one gender—female?

This leads us to focus more specifically on the gender aspects and organization in the school.

Ask Yourself, Have I Noticed:

6. How many of the teaching staff are women and how many are men? What about the custodial staff? Are all the custodial staff men and all the secretarial staff women? What about the principal and assistance principal (if the school has one) are they men or women? How many of the teaching aides or para-professionals are men? How many are women? What type of role models do you think are being presented to children as a result of the gender distribution in the school?

7. While you are noticing the gender distribution of staff and support personnel also make a count of ethnic or racial minority distribution among this group of people. Then think about or find out the gender distribution in the school district's central offices. In the superintendent's office and the central administration how many administrative positions are held by women? How many are held by men? On the board of education of the district, how many men and how many women hold membership? Can you determine their ethnicity or racial affiliations? Again, what does this tell you about equality of representation and the power relationships in society at large and in your local community?

8. When you have observed in classrooms, or walked through the halls of the school, are children usually grouped for activities by gender, i.e. boys are in one line, girls in another? In the classroom have you observed that girls are in one reading group and boys in another? similarly for math? For physical education and playground activities are girls in one area playing their games, while boys are together in another area, playing their games? (Be sure you do not jump to conclusions on the basis of one or two observations when considering these questions.) Further, are children grouping themselves voluntarily into gender or ethnically segregated groups? If you believe this is so, what can teachers and other adults in the school setting do to create opportunities for young children to experience heterogeneous groups?

9. Who participates in school plays and programs at various holidays and festivals? Is it mainly girls? or the majority group? Do minorities get chosen for leading parts, too?

10. What about the school media center or library, does it contain books and other audio-visual materials that reflect the ethnic and racial diversity of our society? Are there stories and pictures about women in various occupations and roles or do the books depict women and girls as homemakers and caregivers, solely? (You may feel that it is important to show men and boys in homemaking settings as well. However, the invisibility of women in the public world of work has been so pervasive, it is important to demonstrate for children that women CAN do more than clean the house and tend the children in the private world of the home.)

11. How recently have teachers and other support staff had a workshop or inservice training in intergroup relations, multicultural education and non-sexist education? And have efforts been exerted to provide administrators and teachers with up-to-date information and research, texts, media and curriculum materials on non-sexist and multicultural education?

Finally, and most crucially, listen to your own voice and observe your own teaching methods:

- Do you frequently assign classroom tasks, activities, reading or math groups, art activities, music lessons, or other group tasks on the basis of gender designations? ethnic group designations? (For example, is it just co-incidence that the "top" reading group is composed of all girls? or all Asians? or the bottom reading group is all boys or all Hispanics?)

- Do you frequently use distinctly different rewards or punishments based on gender or ethnic designations?

- Do you describe children, or their behavior on the basis of gender or racial designation (For example: "Girls just do not push and shove, it is not ladylike!" or "he is so good at running and races, just like ALL those Blacks are?")

- Do you implicitly have different expectations for girls than for boys in academic attainment in your class? for "deportment" and discipline? What about various ethnic and racial minorities, do you hold differing expectations in the cognitive and affective domains for these groups, to the degree that you are stereotyping and not merely taking account of individual differences?

It is not easy to answer the questions posed above with off-the-cuff and facile responses. We urge you to think carefully and thoroughly, examining your feelings and your attitudes, rather than to reply with the taken-for-granted statements that come from what is expected in our daily interactions in schools.

In this regard, another term has come into recent usage to call attention to children that are different and that have learning problems due to their variance from the majority and the mainstream of what could be termed the American educational style. This term is "children at risk" or "high-risk learners." It, too, is an umbrella phrase that educators and government officials are using to label children from lower socio-economic families, from ethnically diverse, immigrant and refugee families, children of families that are now considered homeless, or children of migrant worker families. All of these marginal groups in American society whose children do not fit the traditional, majority, middle class lifestyles, can now fall into a category termed "at risk." But whatever label we give to young children who come into the school and to our classrooms, teachers must feel prepared to develop learning environments that fit their needs and respect their differences.

Multicultural Education as a View of Society from Diverse Ethnic and Gender Perspectives

Raising the ethnic and gender awareness of those who now go into teaching has become an important aspect of most teacher education programs. Teacher preparation across the United States currently includes, within one or more courses, learning about: the history and traditions of American ethnic groups; new immigrant groups; gender and "special" education differences or as some ethnic educators have termed it "single group studies" (Sleeter and Grant, 1988). Additionally, numerous teacher education courses at the graduate level include cross cultural and international education content, with discussions and readings on multicultural education and education for ethnically diverse populations as carried out in other nations. Teacher educators are developing courses and writing textbooks that bring together the new concerns for multicultural, gender, crosscultural and comparative education. An example of this type of offering in a post B.A. degree teacher education is the following:

Teaching in a Multicultural Society

Rationale for the Course

Why should we be concerned about education in a multicultural society? The answer is evident when we consider that never before in history has the world seen such upheaval and mobility in its populations as new waves of immigrants and refugees come to our country. Therefore, we need to give teachers cross-cultural techniques, multiethnic teaching strategies including gender awareness, social science methods, and global perpsectives to cope with what is probably the greatest challenge American education has ever faced.

Topics to be Covered

- Overview of the background and history of cultural pluralism and ethnic diversity in the schools of the United States;
- Discussion of stages in multiculturalism and the links to global perspectives and international human rights affecting education;
- Discussion of implications of integration and desegregation on ethnically diverse populations in American schools;

- Attention to the interactions of ethnicity and race with social class and gender identifications in the school setting;
- Implications of the learning of another language as well as the movement to require English as the "first" language in American schools.

These new developments in teacher education courses heighten the prospective teacher's recognition of the new directions for multicultural education that now encompass integration, multi-lingualism, ethnic studies, pluralistic education, gender awareness and women's studies, and international, crosscultural education. Particularly, we are seeing the influences of women's studies and the growing importance of global awareness impact the teaching of multicultural education. Next, we focus on some especially noteworthy work and writings that have made major contributions to these new directions for multicultural education in global perspectives.

The Development of a Typology: The Stages of Ethnicity

The highly regarded and well-known ethnic scholar, Professor James Banks of the University of Washington, College of Education has been teaching, writing and researching in the field of ethnic education and curriculum development for over two decades. Banks believes that to be able to educate citizens for now and the future, teachers need first to acquire the conceptual framework, skills, and attitudes to view American lifestyles from diverse ethnic perspectives. Banks noted that in the past most teacher training, and thus the practice that resulted in American schools, operated from what he labeled the Anglo-Centric Model. This Anglo-Centric or mainstream-centric model focused primarily on the culture of Anglo-American children, to the exclusion of other ethnic groups. "The Anglo-Centric curriculum, which still exists to varying degrees in most U.S. schools, has harmful consequences for both Anglo-American children and ethnic minorities." (Banks, 1988, p. 35)

To help teachers and teacher educators better understand the dynamics of ethnic identity in a pluralistic society, Banks has developed a typology detailing the stages of ethnicity through which an individual might pass in our American society. This typology is a preliminary ideal-type construct in the Weberian sense and constitutes a set of hypotheses based on theory and research in the field, Banks asserts. These stages should be seen as dynamic and multidimensional with the characteristics of each stage forming a continuum. We give the reader an overview, here, of the typology of the stages of ethnicity. However, we encourage you to refer to the original materials set forth in the book, *Multicultural Education: Theory and Practice,* Second Edition, published by Allyn and Bacon, 1988.

A Typology

Stage 1: Ethnic Psychological Captivity—the individual internalizes the negative and deleterious images of the affiliated group which causes self-rejection and low self-esteem. The individual is ashamed of the group and of identification with this group.

Stage 2: Ethnic Encapsulation—the individual opts for ethnic exclusiveness even to the point of voluntary separatism. During ethnic encapsulation individuals associate primarily with those of the same ethnic group and believe that their group is superior. Individuals, such as Anglo Americans, have internalized the dominant society's myths about the superiority of their ethnic or racial group and the innate inferiority of other ethnic groups. They often choose to live in highly ethnocentric and encapsulated communities.

Stage 3. Ethnic Identity Clarification—the individual is able to clarify personal attitudes and ethnic identity and to develop more positive attitudes toward his or her ethnic group.

Stage 4. Biethnicity—a sense of ethnic identity and the skills needed to participate in both the mainstream culture and the individual's sub-culture evolve, so that the person can function successfully at work, while still holding to one's ethnic ways of life at home.

Stage 5. Multiethnicity and Reflective Nationalism—the individual has a commitment to the affiliated ethnic group while holding empathy and concern for other groups and a broader allegiance to the nation state including idealized values of human rights. Individuals at this stage have cross cultural competency within their own nation, but not a global perspective.

Stage 6. Globalism and Global Competency—the individual has achieved the ideal delicate balance of ethnic, national and global identification, commitments, literacy and behaviors. The individual has internalized the universalistic ethical values and principles of humankind and has the skills and competencies for commitment to a worldwide society. (Banks, 1988 pp. 194–197)

The following pledge, excerpted from material of the Consortium on Rights Development, Graduate School of International Studies, University of Denver, eloquently exemplifies these attitudes and values of a global perspective:

> We, the people of planet Earth, with respect for the dignity of each human life, with concern for future generations, with growing appreciation of our relationship to our environment, with recognition of limits to our resources, and with need for adequate food, air, water, shelter, health, protection, justice and self-fulfillment Hereby declare our INTERDEPENDENCE; And do resolve to work together in peace and in harmony with our environment to enhance the quality of all life everywhere. (Network for Environmental and Economic Responsibility, October, 1988)

Education for an Interdependent World

International educator, sociologist, women's studies scholar and futurist, Professor Elise Boulding certainly embodies the description of the individual who has attained the qualities of James Bank's Stage 6 teacher. She also exemplifies the world citizen who has taken the pledge stated above and lived and worked by its precepts. She has taught, researched and written over the decades of her career as a sociologist, international peace activist and women studies specialist, traveling across the United States and around the world again and again. In one of her most pertinent books for educators and teachers, *Building a Global Civic Culture: Education for an Interdependent World* (Teachers College Press, 1988), Elise

Boulding provides material and strategies for learning and teaching about the worldwide society that IS reality today. She labels this reality the "sociosphere" and she urges teachers to imbue education with local, national and worldwide content. Boulding cautions teachers:

> How do we know about the world? How do we find out what it is like? In the urban and suburban settings of the countries of the North, and for some elites of the South, children grow into adulthood without ever discovering anything about the physical and social environment beyond their own personal daily path, except through programmed secondary sources such as television, radio, the telephone, the computer, and of course, books. They live in technologically shielded settings that cut them off from feedback about the larger environment in which they live. In fact, it is considered progress NOT to have to bother with getting or dealing with that feedback. (Boulding, 1988, p. 77)

In her book on educating for our interdependent world, Boulding calls attention to the importance of conflict management in the face of wide-ranging diversity and cultural pluralism in so many of the modern nation states. She presents strategies and methods for developing skills that are needed to deal with this diversity and the conflicts that it brings. She believes that no one society can create or impose THE universal social order; therefore, it is incumbent on societies to find creative ways of working together which acknowledge our human diversity and can maintain an overall level of peaceableness, avoiding destructive strategies that deny our differences (Boulding, 1988)

Some of the strategies and techniques that Boulding outlines are derived from what we already know about what works well in our local schools and communities; techniques such as problem-solving competencies, skills of coping with stress, confidence in our own integrity, respect for others, and the creative use of the social imagination. She calls to our attention how problems of knowing in a complex, highly technologized culture hold teachers to presenting knowledge in linear, rationalized, procedurally driven thinking modes. Therefore, she calls upon teachers to consider intuitive modes of addressing social problems and the use of skills of the imagination, providing a number of examples of how the imagination can be used to deepen our understanding of complex social phenomena by exercises in imagining the future.

From Boulding's own community and teaching experiences she draws the suggestions that teachers and their students become involved in intergovernmental and nongovernmental networks from the base of their own community. This could be considered another dimension or an extension of the community involvement we described in earlier chapters. For example, teachers can assign children in upper elementary school classes to check with family members and ask about international organizations to which they belong. Teachers can provide the model for their students by discussing the international organizations and their functions that the teachers participate in, as well as, the nongovernmental and commercial organization to which they belong. This could include: church membership, service clubs, the Chamber of Commerce, business and professional organizations, sports associations, the YMCA or YWCA, scouting groups, and so on. Children, as well as teachers, can check the school library and the local libraries to document the history and current

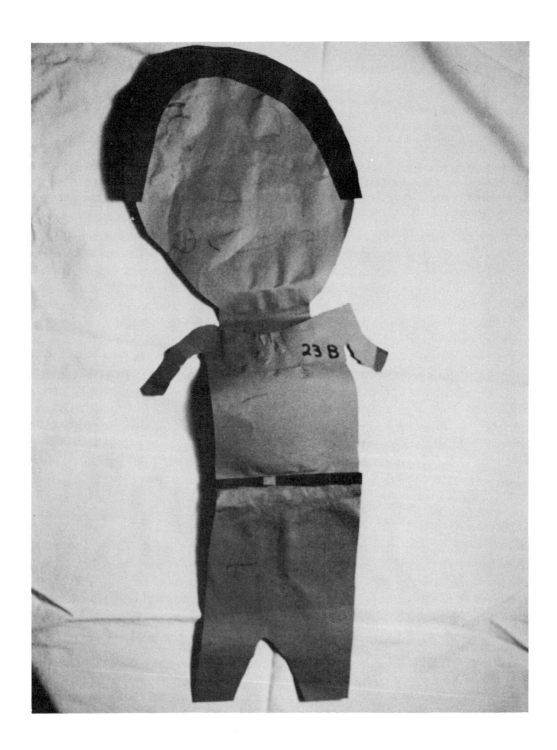

activities of the organizations they have uncovered through these investigations. This could lead to a series of projects around the subject of "your community in the world and the world in your community" that contains numerous possibilities for learning activities.

However, one of the most creative, unique and provocative strategies for encouraging education for an interdependent world Boulding offers us is the "Portfolio of Global Experience." Teachers should be stimulated to fill out this questionnaire initially and then develop techniques for using the Portfolio with students. Boulding notes in the preface to the Portfolio that it is useful in understanding global education to build on the background of world experience and perceptions of the planet that you already have. All of us, even young children, live in a worldwide culture today, so we have developed perceptions and attitudes about the peoples of the earth. The "portfolio" which is actually a questionnaire contains specific sections that ask the respondent to list the following:

- residential mobility, i.e. home addresses where one has lived for at least six months since time of birth;
- subcultures, such as ethnic, racial, religious, political that one has been a part of or has known;
- travel experiences to regions of this country or to other countries;
- languages other than English spoken or used;
- media experiences that have shaped one's attitudes about the world;
- persons in one's life who have shaped one's understanding of the world including public personages from the media and political life;
- events in one's life that have impacted one's world view.

Elise Boulding's writings bring to education new resources and new thinking on education for a global society, for women's roles and empowerment in that global society and for the importance of dealing with differences in every aspect of the school curriculum. As Margaret Mead has urged us, we should work towards attaining a world order in which social conflicts can be handled by less than ultimate forms of threat and counterthreat. Now, we have no choice in the matter. All societies must work to solve these social conflicts or witness the end of human cultures as we have known them. Elise Boulding carries on the work and traditions of Margaret Mead in building "the global civic culture" through education at every age and grade level.

These then are the current influences on multicultural education and education for dealing with differences. Formerly, multiethnic education and ethnic studies included just the study and understanding of the various ethnic and racial groups in the United States. It was deeply impacted by the concerns for pluralistic education, ethnic diversity and prejudice reduction and so broadened to multicultural education. Which in turn, was extended to an awareness of gender differences, women's studies and the inclusion of physical and psychological difference. Finally, multicultural education has encompassed a world view to recognize the necessity for teaching all children to live in a global society and a worldwide culture.

Future Directions for Multicultural Education
Merging with Global Education and Gender Studies

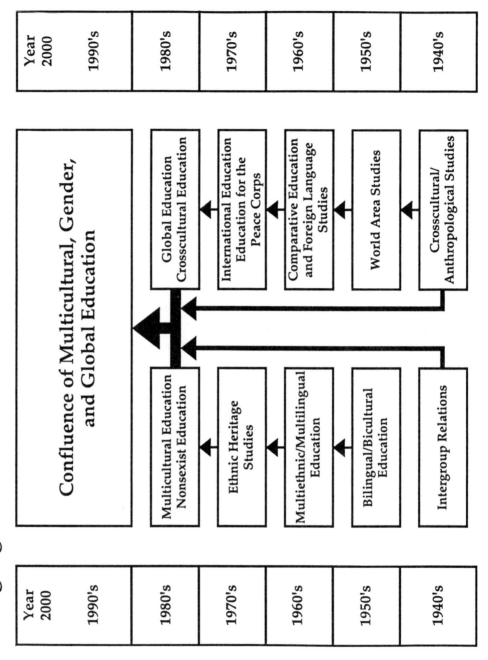

	Year 2000	1990's	1980's	1970's	1960's	1950's	1940's

Confluence of Multicultural, Gender, and Global Education

Global Education
Crosscultural Education

International Education
Education for the Peace Corps

Comparative Education and Foreign Language Studies

World Area Studies

Crosscultural/ Anthropological Studies

Multicultural Education
Nonsexist Education

Ethnic Heritage Studies

Multiethnic/Multilingual Education

Bilingual/Bicultural Education

Intergroup Relations

	Year 2000	1990's	1980's	1970's	1960's	1950's	1940's

Tips for Teaching: An Emerging Respect for Diversity

What implications do the international, crosscultural influences have for teaching and the curriculum in American schools? We believe that acceptance of international inputs will provide a bridge between global and multicultural education. Just as global education has played its part in the curriculum since the 1950's, so will multicultural education continue to be a conspicuous influence in the social sciences and in all other areas of school program. But where these two dimensions of contemporary educational practice join to produce a new awareness of local, regional, national and transnational linkages, the impact will be startling. The combination of multicultural education and global education cannot help but produce striking changes in the nature and implementation of the American school curriculum. Here now are some additional suggestions for incorporating a growing respect for diversity in your daily teaching.

Languages in My Life Questionnaire

To find out if the children in your class speak a different language or dialect than standard English in their homes with parents, siblings, relatives and friends, use the following questions or develop your own variation of this technique to fit your classes.

1. What language or languages did you first speak with your family before you came to this school?
2. Where does this language (or dialect) come from? — country, region or nationality?
3. What language or languages do you mainly use with your family and friends? a) When I speak to my mother and father, I speak _____ . b) When I speak to my brothers and sisters, I speak _____ . c) When I speak to my relatives like aunts and uncles, I speak _____ .
4. What languages other than English do you hear spoken in your neighborhood? Do you ever see signs or notices in your neighborhood in languages other than English? If so, find out about these languages and tell us in school what they are.

As a teacher you may be surprised how many of the children in your class and in your school are exposed to differing languages and dialects, and different forms of written languages. Think of what rich resources a questionnaire like "Languages in My Life" can uncover for you, the teacher, to use in developing multicultural and global education in your programs.

Materials That Combine Multicultural, Global and Gender Awareness

More than ever before, outstanding and stimulating materials are at hand—in some of the most unlikely places—that combine aspects of multiculturalism, gender awareness, and an international perspective. Here are several categories of such curriculum material. Innovative teachers of young children are constantly alert to obtaining teaching aides and these are just examples of what are now on the shelves of local bookstores and variety stores, or available in professional organizations, magazines, journals, newsletters, and even the daily newspaper.

1. Atlases—paperback versions. This particular atlas was found in the section of a bookstore labeled "Women's Studies." Title: *Women of the World Atlas* by Joni Seager and Ann Olson, published by Pluto Press (Pan Books, 1986). This unique atlas contains 40 charts on the conditions of the world's women, including educational attainment data and the consequences of education or the lack of it upon the women of the world. The material can be adapted for upper elementary school levels, although it has been prepared for adult reading.

2. Calendars—a striking calendar with large black and white photographs of famous women, their memorable quotations, and brief biographies, is titled *"Remarkable Women, 1989"* published by Golden Turtle Press (1619 Shattuck Avenue, Berkely, CA 94700). This calendar was purchased in a variety store, but might also be found in the local supermarket or bookstore where calendars are usually sold. This stunning calendar includes vignettes on Rachel Carson, Sojourner Truth, Anna Pavlova, Helen Keller, Beatrix Potter, Susan B. Anthony, Golda Meir, and other internationally recognized, famous women in the arts and letters.

3. Newsletters and Journals for Educators—that are dedicated to combining the concerns of multicultural education, women's studies and global education. An outstanding newsletter titled *Global Pages* is published by the Immaculate Heart College Center, (10951 West Pico Boulevard, Suite 2021, Los Angeles, California, 90024). There are two issues a year. This invaluable curriculum newsletter provides teachers with information, strategies, teaching techniques, resources and supportive reassurance in their quest to teach with feminist and global perspectives. For example, the *Global Pages* issue of October–December, 1988, featured a cover page poster with the quotation "Both global and multicultural studies should 'give voice' to those who have been excluded from a curriculum dominated by Western, white and male traditions." Currently, *Global Pages* is distributed free of charge.

Specialized educational publications devoted to multicultural, non-sexist, and global interests in curriculum development and teacher education—a well organized, thorough, timely and outstanding publication for teachers, educators and administrators is *Multicultural Leader* published quarterly by the Educational Materials and Services Center, (144 Railroad Avenue, Suite 107, Edmonds, Washington, 98020). Although this professional publication has a subscription fee, it provides teachers with the most current thinking in the field of multicultural education (including women's studies and international education), excellent book reviews, research reports, and news of multicultural education abroad.

Published in Britain since 1982, the international journal targeted for teachers working in multicultural and multiracial schools is titled *Multicultural Teaching; To Combat Racism in School and Community*. It is edited by Gillian Klein, the author of *The Scrapbooks* series that we discussed in a previous chapter and is available from

Trentham Books (151 Etruria Road, Stoke-on-Trent, Staffordshire, STl 5 NS, England). The "Statement of Purpose" of *Multicultural Teaching* informs readers that it is concerned with all aspects of teaching and learning in a multicultural society. Each issue consists of professional practice, discussion of its aims and purposes and examples of its achievements. This journal also includes reviews of important new books and resources in Britain, the United States, Canada, Australia, European and Southeast Asian nations. *Multicultural Teaching* is representative of the dynamic new publications that are arising across the world to meet the challenge of informing teachers and other educators about exemplary practice that includes international, feminist and multicultural dimensions. There is a subscription fee for this journal which is published four times a year.

Summary

In this chapter we have traced trends and influences that have affected the emergence of multicultural education. We have attempted to predict where multicultural education is headed as we bring together multiculturalism in the United States with international perspectives and gender issues. Multicultural education is essential for a pluralistic society. Human nature cries out for personal dignity and recognition. This is vital for learning. Every child possesses roots—roots in a family, in a neighborhood, in a community, in a region, in a nation and finally in humanity—in the global existence of peoplehood. Through multicultural education as we have come to define it, we can find honor and dignity for each individual. It is the contribution that teachers can and must give to children.

References

Banks, James A. *Multiethnic Education: Theory and Practice*. Second Edition. Newton, Mass: Allyn and Bacon, 1988.

——— *Teaching Strategies for Ethnic Studies*. 4th edition, Newton, Mass: Allyn and Bacon, 1987.

Banks, J. A. and Banks, C. (editors) *Multicultural Education: Issues and Perspectives*. Newton, Mass: Allyn and Bacon, 1989.

Banks, J. A. and Lynch, J. (editors) *Multicultural Education in Western Societies*. London: Cassell, 1986

Boulding, Elise. *Building a Global Civic Cultural: Education for an Interdependent World*. New York: Teachers College Press, 1988.

Hernandez, Hilda. *Multicultural Education: A Teacher's Guide to Content and Process*. Columbus: Merrill Publishing Company, 1989

Issues of *Multicultural Leader*. Edmonds, Wash.: Educational Materials and Services Center.

Issues of *Multicultural Teaching*. To Combat Racism in School and Community. Stoke-On-Trent, England: Trentam Books.

Lynch, James. *Prejudice Reductions and the Schools*. London: Cassell, 1987.

McLaren, Peter. *Life in Schools*. New York: Longman, 1989.

Sleeter, C. and Grant, C. *Making Choices for Multicultural Education;* Five Approaches to Race, Class and Gender. Columbus: Merrill Publishing Co. 1988.

Activities for Recognizing Ethnicity, Social Class and Gender in the Elementary School

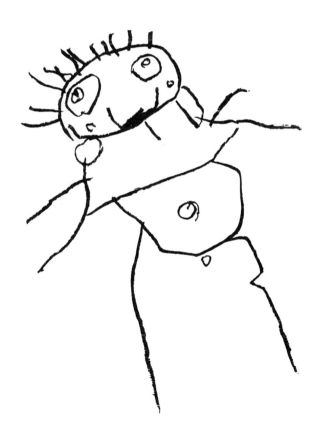

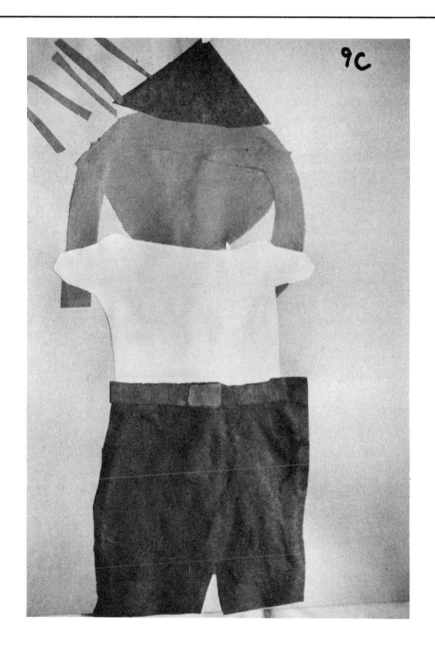

LET'S LOOK AT OURSELVES

Introduction

Obtain a large mirror, sturdy enough to place safely in a prominent position in the classroom. Use the mirror to initiate discussion among the children of individual characteristics like skin, hair, and eye color, general physical stature, shape of faces, texture of hair and so on. It is very important that the teacher acknowledge differences but keep the conversation firmly on a positive basis with approving comments, so that no child feels demeaned or devalued for his or her physical characteristics.

We realize that this is a rather innovative activity for teachers of young children, since, for so many years, we have stressed similarities not differences among children. Teachers have been urged to ignore differences in skin color, hair texture, size and stature to the point that discussions such as we are suggesting here were virtually taboo. We feel this attitude is misguided; children recognize differences at an early age—especially skin color, hair textures, height and weight.

Objectives:
1. To help young children discover their own unique physical characteristics in comparison with other children. Some young children have few opportunities to look in a mirror and find out what they really look like. In some homes, mirrors are placed at heights appropriate for adults, and young children never get to look at themselves in the mirror or are not encouraged to find out what they look like.
2. To encourage children to feel their physical characteristics—skin, eyes, hair, figure—are attractive, accepted by others and equally as pretty or handsome as other children their age.
3. To create a general atmosphere of acceptance and recognition for each child in the group.
4. To provide preparation and background for futher activities that focus on self-awareness, self-identity and self-acceptance.

Materials:

One large mirror that can be placed easily in the classroom.

Procedure:

1. Place the mirror in a central and convenient location in the classroom. Gather the children around the mirror in a semicircle formation. If you have a class size of more than 18 to 20 students, it is suggested that you conduct this activity in two or even three groups of children. It is important that each child have a turn at viewing himself

or herself in the mirror, full-length and for enough time to really examine and consider physical characteristics. If you have a highly active child or several children with short attention spans, plan to have such children included in smaller groups of only 6 to 8 members. An average-sized group for this activity is about 10 children.

2. Begin the activity by having the children look at the teacher closely, observing skin color, hair color and texture, eye color, stature and so on.

3. Have each child in the group stand in front of the mirror and examine his or her features. Encourage the child to comment on details such as skin color, eye color, hair color and texture, with comments and reactions from the other children. Again we stress that the tone and atmosphere of the group discussion has to be kept on a positive and supportive level.

4. After each child in the group has had the opportunity to view and examine his or her features in the mirror and for the group to react and comment, be sure to close the discussion with positive and approving comments.

5. Move on to one (or more) of the suggested follow-up activities as soon as the classroom schedule permits.

Follow-up Activities:

1. Have available magazines, scissors, paste and plain sheets of paper, 11 × 14 inches or longer. Tell the children to search through the magazines for people with different faces, differing heights and figures, different hair styles and so on. Have each child make a collage or make one large collage to which the group of children contribute. On a large sheet of chart paper you can put a title such as "People Come in All Shapes and Sizes" or "Let's Look at People" or another title you compose, and have each child paste the pictures chosen on the large mural or collage.

2. Obtain a number of well-conceived and well-written children's books on multi-ethnic concepts. Read these books with the children or let them peruse the pictures themselves. For example, the classic story of a mixed, black-white family, by Arnold Adoff, *Black Is Brown Is Tan* (New York: Harper and Row, 1973) provides sensitive and insightful ways of portraying young children of various ethnic backgrounds. Look for authors and illustrators, such as Ezra Jack Keats and Ann Laris, who are deeply concerned with a child's positive self-image. These books will encourage youngsters to become aware of their own racial and ethnic heritage in positive and useful ways which will bring meaningful content to the multicultural curriculum.

"IT'S ME!" SELF-PORTRAIT COLLAGES

Introduction:

This activity can be particularly useful in revealing children's personalities and self-concepts. Whether you have engaged in the "Let's Look at Ourselves" activity or not, having the children create self portraits will prove a meaningful classroom experience that has subtle ethnic and racial implications if you are sensitive to their existence.

Objectives:
1. To provide an open setting for children to express their self-perceptions.
2. To provide opportunities for small muscle activities, such as cutting, pasting, designing and organizing with scissors, paste and colored construction paper.
3. To allow children a means of expressing their inner feelings about themselves physically and emotionally.
4. To create an opportunity for the teacher and other adults involved with the children to gain new insights into personality development, self-identity and self-concept.

Procedure:

1. Give each child a piece of construction paper, at least 8″ × 11″ in size, of neutral color, such as manila, pale green or white. Also provide scissors and paste, but urge the children to put away all crayons and pencils. Place additional pieces of colored construction paper, large and small, scraps and full sheets in a convenient location on tables for easy access.

2. Instruct the children that the purpose of this game is to create a portrait of themselves using as many pieces, rather than colors, of paper as they choose. Suggest that they design the features, body parts and clothing by using scissors and then pasting the parts together, rather than trying to draw themselves. (The point of this activity is to reveal self-concepts through construction paper collages rather than conventionally drawn self-portraits.)

Follow-up Activities:

You can collect the collages and display them in your classroom. But be sure to examine each self-portrait carefully. Here are some aspects to look for:

1. What colors of construction paper has the child chosen to represent skin color? Does this accurately reflect the child's racial or ethnic background, or is it some bizarre color such as green or purple? Psychologists have pointed out that children who wish to deny their racial identity and skin color often portray themselves with bizarre colors rather than in the authentic hue.

2. How large or small has the child portrayed the total figure created? Is the image small or located on one side of the paper or does it fill up most of the sheet? The size of the total figure can be revealing about the child's self-concept?

3. How detailed is the child's self-portrait? How accurate and true-to-life are these details? You will find some children create collages which are remarkably accurate and detailed, while other children put together pictures of themselves which appear far-fetched and bizarre. Notice, also, whether the child creates only the face or head or develops a collage including the entire body and perhaps even objects, a scene or pets.

PROMOTING ETHNIC AWARENESS AND SELF-IDENTITY
WITH YOUNG CHILDREN

Introduction:

Once teachers have established the awareness required for stimulating multicultural education in their classrooms, how can they communicate this to the children? Here is a strategy to promote ethnic awareness and self-identity among young children. Before a child can be helped to a higher degree of self-acceptance, the teacher must accept that child. To this end, a short list of questions was drawn up to begin a process of discovering what preconceived ideas the teacher holds about the ethnicity of the students. Then a longer set of questions was composed to ask children to think about who they are and how they are alike and different from others.

Following the questionnaire for teachers, we have suggested using Dr. Seuss' delightful story, *The Sneeches,* as an ice-breaker to get the children started thinking about differences and how they are viewed. Next we introduce the questionnaire for children. When asking the questions, the teacher should be as open as possible and accept whatever the children say. A wide range of answers is possible.

It is important in the process of helping children with self-acceptance to reinforce the positive aspects of each child's personality. This is not an easy task, and the very child within whom it is most difficult to find favorable assets is probably the one with the greatest needs.

Teacher Pre-Test:

Ask yourself the following questions as they apply to each of your students. Then compare your answers with each student's answers about him/herself.

1. What do you call this student? (Anglo, Black, Asian, Hispanic, Italian, Jewish, Muslim? Troublemaker, Angel, Teacher's Pet, Show-off? etc.)
2. What do you think he/she calls him/herself?
3. From where do you think his/her family may have come?
4. Do you consider this student to be light or dark in complexion? Compared to what?
5. If this student respects your opinion of him/her, what effect would your good or bad image of him/her have on his/her self-concept.

Procedure for Using the Sneeches:

1. Read to the class the following story: *The Sneeches,* by Dr. Seuss (Geisel, Theordore Seuss) New York: Random House, 1961.
2. Discuss with the class the following questions:
   a. What was the importance of the stars, or were the stars important?
      Possible Answer: The stars were a way to tell the Sneeches apart—good/bad, in-group/out-group, .
   b. Was having a star good or bad?
      Possible Answer: Good at first, then bad, then at the end it didn't matter.

c. How was it decided that a star was good or bad?
Possible Answer: The Sneeches decided as a group—especially the ones "who had stars at first."

d. How was the problem of stars or no-stars finally resolved?
Possible Answer: The Sneeches got so mixed up that they no longer knew which ones had stars before and which didn't.

e. What is this story, *The Sneeches,* really about?
Possible Answer: Discrimination based on superficial or surface appearances.

Questionnaire for Children:

Ask your students the following questions. You may wish to do it as a class discussion or you may wish to ask the questions individually and in confidence.

Part I—About You

1. What kind of person are you? (boy? girl? tall? short? Black? White? Irish? smart? pretty? noisy? plain?)
2. Why do you look the way you look?
3. Why don't you look different?
4. Are you an American? What does that mean?
5. What kind of American are you? (Mexican American, Anglo American, etc.)
6. Are you Chinese, Italian, Irish, etc.?
7. Why or why not?
8. What are you?
9. What are your parents?
10. Where did your ancestors come from?
11. If your family speaks or could speak a language other than English, what is it?
12. What color is your skin? Is it light? dark?

Part II—About Others

1. What are some other kinds of people called:
   a. in your school?
   b. in your town or city?
   c. in your country?
   d. in the world?

2. How can you tell when a person is just like you? Do you know anyone like you? Describe them.

3. Think of someone who is different from you. Describe them. How can you tell when a person is different from you? What kinds of things make them different?

4. What things do you use to decide whether a person is like you or different from you?

5. Can you think of anyone who may think *you* are different? What might make them think you are different?

6. How do you feel about being pretty much like someone else? How do you feel about being different from someone else?

7. Is it okay to like someone who is different from you?

8. What would the world be like if we were all the same?

DEVELOPING AN ETHNIC CHART STORY

Introduction:

Public school teachers tend to shy away from dealing with complex social concepts and controversial issues in the earliest years of school. Ideas of ethnicity and pluralism, as well as sexism and desegregation, are frequently considered too advanced to discuss in daily activities such as "Show and Tell." But children must be prepared to live in a multicultural society, and the early childhood classroom offers an opportunity to provide them with pride in their heritage. Then children can extend this sense of belonging and self-acceptance to others.

This activity presents techniques for teaching about ethnicity, pluralism and nonsexist attitudes. It also provides opportunities for learning left-to-right direction in reading word recognition, spelling sentence structure and creative writing, plus providing art activities and social development.

Objectives:
1. To introduce young children to aspects of ethnicity and pluralism in their personal and family lives.
2. To develop awareness in young children of ethnicity, family heritage and sex-role behaviors in daily living.
3. To help young children recognize that all people have a heritage and traditions.

Materials:

Chart paper and magic markers.

Procedure:

1. Introduce the concepts of ethnicity, heritage, family descent and family traditions through writing an experience story on chart paper or on the chalkboard. The teacher writes down the words of the story, but the children as a group provide the content, words, sentences and sequence of the story.
2. It is useful to "break the ice" and help children understand the terms ethnicity, heritage, descent and nationality. The teacher can accomplish this by describing his or her own heritage or by giving examples from members of the class. For example, "Last week Carl told us about the fine family birthday party he went to. Do you remember that he said it was celebrated in *real* Italian style? Carl's father is of Italian descent or heritage." Or, "Remember when Jenny's mother brought us some delicious cakes called baklava? Jenny's mother is of Greek ethnicity or background. Her mother knows how to make the traditional dessert many Greek-American people like to eat—baklava."

3 Begin your ethnic chart story by asking the children if they know what heritage, nationality, tradition or descent their mothers and/or fathers come from.

4. As the children respond to the inquiries about ethnic heritage and family nationality or descent, write down their answers. Some children may state that they do not know about their family heritage. Assure them that this is all right and encourage them to find out by asking their parents and relatives. Other children may describe several ethnicities or traditions within their families. Still other children may appear confused about their family heritage. Reassure the children on this point by saying that many people in America today may have lost contact with their ancestors, but it is interesting to know about one's heritage.

5. Compose a final form of the ethnic chart story by bringing together the information and ideas generated by the children's discussion. Read over the story with the children several times in the next day or two to refresh and reinforce the ideas and interest in the topic.

6. A day or so after developing the ethnic chart story, distribute an "Ethnic Family Tree" handout to each child. Ask them to take the sheet home and have their parents help them fill in the blanks. Request that the children return the worksheet to class, so that the group can revise and rewrite the ethnic chart story.

7. When most of the "Ethnic Family Tree" handouts have been returned, write a new chart story of the class that includes the information collected by the children.

Follow-up Activities:

1. The ethnic chart story and the family tree ditto sheet should stimulate much interest and discussion among the children about ancestors, grandparents and family traditions. Since the study of families is a major topic in the early childhood curriculum, this focus on ethnicity and family heritage can bring new dimensions and new interest to the traditional study of "the family" in kindergartens, pre-schools and primary grade levels. We should also emphasize the pluralistic nature of our culture by highlighting the many ethnicities and nationalities the children's families represent. Further, many children will find evidence of mixed heritages and ethnic groups in their families. Parents and other relatives will be interested in contributing to the classroom study of family heritage. This can lead to field trips and to inviting resource persons into the classroom. The study of ethnicity and family heritage brings meaningful new content to early childhood education.

2. To help teachers instill multicultural and nonsexist attitudes in the classroom, refer to the discussion in Chapter 3 of this book. This background can be helpful in stimulating the children to respond to activities such as the ethnic chart story and the ethnic heritage family tree.

Ethnic Heritage Family Tree

I Came From
_____

Dad Came From
_____

Mom Came From
_____

Grandpa Came From
_____

Grandma Came From
_____

Grandpa Came From
_____

Grandma Came From
_____

Some of My Other Ancestors Came From

_____

_____

_____

_____

TEACHING ABOUT ETHNICITY AND GENDER AWARENESS
WITH PUPPETS

Introduction:

Why teach about ethnic and gender awareness? Whether there is considerable diversity of ethnic cultures within the local community or hardly any, it is important that children become aware of some facts:

1. People have differing practices and beliefs influenced by their ethnicity and by their gender.
2. "Different" does not mean "peculiar."
3. People do not have to express or display their ethnic preferences even though the backgrounds for these heritages exist in their family.
4. Gender differences can also be seen as equally important and valuable in society.

Objectives:
1. To recognize that all Americans have ethnic heritages.
2. To recognize that not all people practice ethnic customs and beliefs, and that these customs can be related to gender expectations.
3. To trace students' own ethnic backgrounds.
4. To locate on a map or globe at least one country from which students' ancestors came.
5. To recognize that "different" is not "peculiar."

Time:

Several 30-minute class periods.

Materials:

Puppets (at least some of whom represent males and females), and stimulus materials such as slides, videotapes, or pictures of classrooms in which the boys and girls represent various racial and ethnic groups; or use the "Family Tree" ditto handout from the previous "Developing An Ethnic Chart Story" activity; map or globe; paper and crayons.

Procedure:

1. Help the students create a puppet show to introduce the terms "ethnicity" and the term "gender." If you feel that the children are not familiar with these two, now-popular, social terms, illustrate and develop their meanings by showing a film, a videotape, slides or pictures. An example of media material that features information about both ethnicity and gender is the well-known book-record-film, *Free to Be Me and You,* featuring Marlo Thomas, and (the then) very young Michael Jackson. Point out that all people have ethnic backgrounds and a gender identity. Explain that the students are going to look into some of the heritages of their ancestors as well as the impact of being a man or a woman in different cultures. After initiating and preparing the students, write the puppet show script. (You can adapt the same techniques from the "Developing An Ethnic Chart Story" activity here).

2. Produce the puppet show with students from the class and other students viewing the results. Hold a discussion to determine if all the children have grasped the concepts of "ethnicity" and "gender"

3. Invite other classes and their teachers to view your puppet show. Then hold another discussion. Try to stress that people can be viewed in many ways. No two people are exactly alike; they have varying figures, shapes, sizes, skin colors and ethnic backgrounds. Being unique is good—different is not peculiar.

THE MULTIETHNIC DOLLHOUSE PROJECT

Introduction:

Young children delight in observing, collecting and playing with dollhouses and doll-sized furniture. An exciting variation on the traditional dollhouse hobby is to create a multi-ethnic dollhouse, made up of rooms representing differing ethnic heritages in American society.

For example, one early childhood teacher was able to interest various parents and resource persons in putting together a dollhouse with rooms representing differing cultures. One room, representing the Oriental tradition, had gold paper on the wall, mirrors, model Japanese furniture and dolls dressed in Kabuki robes. Another room was outfitted in Polish tradition with wall decorations, paper cutouts and hand-painted ornaments. Mexican American culture was represented by clay and tin dolls in costumes of the Hispanic tradition. The possibilities for heritage rooms are manifold and very intriguing to young children.

Objectives:
1. To stimulate interest and activities in learning about the multi-ethnic traditions of America.
2. To utilize a beloved custom of childhood, the dollhouse and doll-sized furniture, for learning about ethnicity.
3. To provide a vehicle for parents' and other adults' involvement in multi-ethnic education.

Materials:

As suggested by the craft projects that evolve.

Procedure:

1. Begin an inquiry, either informally or through written notices, to parents, teachers and other resource people in the school community, asking if they can help create sample dollhouse rooms of various ethnic heritages.
2. Once you have located a number of interested parties, assemble the Multi-ethnic Dollhouse in your classroom, in the library or multi-media center or in another appropriate location.
3. Have the children make contributions to the various rooms in the dollhouse. You may want to use your resource persons or parents to demonstrate ethnic crafts such as the Polish paper cutouts or hand-painted ornaments. Developing a simplified variation of craft project may be more feasible for young children.
4. Discuss the significance of the items in the various ethnic room settings with the children.

114

Follow-up Activities:

1. Writing thank-you notes to parents and resource persons for their contributions to the Multi-ethnic Dollhouse is a way to involve language arts activities in this project.

2. Group-dictated chart stories and written descriptions of the Multi-ethnic Dollhouse also bring language skills into the multi-ethnic education project.

DON'T JUDGE A PACKAGE BY ITS WRAPPINGS

Introduction:

The activity begins with two simple demonstrations, showing children that things—i.e., packages and books—are not what they might seem to be at first encounter. The analogy here is that the same holds true with people. The teacher prepares two packages or presents, one beautifully wrapped in enticing paper with colorful ribbons, the other package should be plainly tied up with string or twine. The contents of the beautifully wrapped package should contain items of little value, things that children would not find much fun, while the contents of the plainly wrapped package should be something your group of children would highly value.

Keep in mind the same considerations as you choose three books, unfamiliar to the children, to display in your classroom. These books should be of different types, on differing subjects, and of various reading levels. Take care to choose books whose covers do not necessarily indicate their contents or subject.

Objectives:

1. To help children understand that they cannot always judge people or things by first appearance or initial impressions.
2. To provide a springboard for discussion about appearances, attitudes and values.
3. To familiarize students with words such as prejudice, dislikes, differences, distrust and appearances and what they mean when applied to themselves and to others.
4. To provide opportunities for children to examine their own identities and to compare their families and their preferences with children of other families.
5. To create opportunities for role-playing in which personal likes and dislikes are expressed.

Materials:

Student handout, "All About Me—And Others"; two wrapped boxes and something to put in them; three (specially-chosen) books.

Procedure:

1. Introduce the activity with the packages and the books, encouraging the children to comment on their choices. Make an accounting of the children's preferences for the packages and for the books, putting the results in a large piece of chart paper or on the board for everyone to see.
2. Open the packages with the children and let them express their reactions to the contents. Then do the same thing for the books.

3. Relate the situation of the packages and the books to a similar situation of people. Use terms such as alike, similar, prejudice, dislike or distrust with regard to people. Ask the children why one might distrust another person if one doesn't know that person. As the children discuss their ideas and feelings, try to list as many as you can on the board or on chart paper for later reference.

4. Pass out the student questionnaire, "All About Me—and Others." Have the children complete the questionnaire. Discuss the children's responses. Role-play some of the following suggested situations.

   a. A new child who appears different from the other children is placed in your class or in your group. How do you react?

   b. A new child comes into your group, and the other children are not accepting and being helpful to the newcomer.

   c. A new child comes into your group, and the other children are accepting and being helpful to the newcomer. Be sure to encourage group discussion.

5. Collect the questionnaires and read them over. The responses are certain to provide the teacher with important insights and useful information about the children in the class.

Follow-up Activities:

1. Return the questionnaires to the children and have them discuss their responses and reactions several days later. See if they come to the realization of what the demonstration with the packages and the books was attempting to do.

2. Ask the children how they responded to the item "I am." Some will have put their name in the blank provided; others will have responded with their age or sex. What responses were made to this item? Categorize the responses. What insights does this provide about the individual child's self-concept and sense of self-identity?

3. Do the same thing for the items, "My mother," "My father" and "My family is." Many children will respond with proper names or family names. Other children will list adjectives such as "nice" or "happy" or state an age. Occasionally, children respond with ethnic or religious adjectives like Christian, Jewish, Mexican, etc.

4. Go through the entire questionnaire, even if it takes two or three sessions on different days. Allow the children to state the various responses they have made to the questionnaire items, comparing and contrasting the individual responses. You will find that you know much more about the children in your classroom after using this questionnaire.

All about Me—and Others

Name _____

Date _____

I am _____

My mother is _____

My father is _____

My family is _____

My favorite food is _____

My favorite TV show is _____

I feel good when _____

I feel bad when _____

I like to _____

I don't like to _____

Pretend

that a child who is different from me comes to this school.

That child might be _____

That child might like _____

Tell several things you might learn about that person.

_____

_____

_____

I chose package number _____ because_____

I chose book number _____ because _____

Name stephany

Date March 9

I am The same color as my friend.

My mother is older than me.

My father will let me go on scholl trips.

My family is My family Has Four people in it.

My favorite food is Mexacan

My favorite TV show is the price is right

I feel good when I feed my Dog

I feel bad when I Brack my glasses

I like to play

I don't like having to wash my hair

PRETEND _____

that a child who is different from me comes to this school.

That child might be like me

That child might like to whach tv.

Tell several things that you might learn about that person.

That person might have The same
color of hair and skin and He might
Be very nice

I chose package 2 because it looked pritty

I chose book 1 because it looks good

Name _Suzy A._

Date _March 9_

I am _eight years old and my name is Suzy_

My mother _is 36 years old and her name is Donna_

My father _is 38 years old and his name is Jim_

My family is _going to go on a trip_

My favorite food is _Steak Maceronie._

My favorite TV show is _Happy days_

I feel good when _I win a prize_

I feel bad when _I get yelled at_

I like to _do art, swim, gimnasticks._

I don't like having to _clean up the Kitchen_

PRETEND _____

that a child who is different from me comes to this school.

That child might be _from a diffrent country_

That child might like _the things I like_

Tell several things that you might learn about that person.

his family, language, hobbies, age, what Kind of clothing he likes to ware

I chose package _B_ because _of the wrapping_

I chose book _C_ because _I like the book_

Name Brad O.

Date March 9

I am American

My mother is nice

My father is nice

My family is is nice

My favorite food is Hamberger

My favorite TV show is on the rocks

I feel good when i have somewon to play with.

I feel bad when some one is mene to me.

I like to Ski

I don't like having to pick up My room

PRETEND

that a child who is different from me comes to this school.

That child might be press Diffretly

That child might like To play footBall

Tell several things that you might learn about that person.

He Might tell Me a other longuage. He Might teach me a sport. He Might Be nicer then others

I chose package 1 because it is a suprise

I chose book 2 because it is good

121

LINING UP: AN ACTIVITY FOR GENDER AWARENESS

Introduction:

It has just been our habit in the kindergarten and primary levels to have children line-up in a girls' line and in a boys' line. It is such a taken-for-granted and unquestioned way of organizing children for centuries now, that no one considers the sexist nature of such a mundane activity. This activity for gender awareness calls upon teachers of young children to revolutionize these practices of "lining up" children by sex, when going from location to location, within the room, the school building or on field trips outside the school.

Objectives:
Students will begin to realize that other categories for social organization exist than solely gender identification.

Procedure:

When the occasion arises to have the children "line up" for situations such as dismissals, going to another classroom, moving from one part of the classroom to another, going to the lavatory if it is outside the classroom, etc.; develop other strategies than saying the usual "all the girls in one line, all the boys in another." Try lining children up by the colors in their clothing or the letters of the alphabet—all the "A's" to "M's" in one line and the "N's" to "Z's" in the other line.

Follow-up Activities:

You can enjoy being creative to see how many clever ways you and your colleagues can come up with to replace the traditional boys' and girls' "lines." Have a contest? Vote on the most clever and unique technique. Think up an unusual and appropriate prize for the winner, too. It will make your teaching more interesting and creative.

Section B
FOR MIDDLE ELEMENTARY LEVELS

MY ETHNIC NEIGHBORHOOD

Introduction:

In Part I of this book, we discussed the pluralistic nature of American society. We pointed out that in every school, in every classroom, there are children who represent a number of ethnic groups in American life. Too often teachers are prone to think that since all the pupils in their class appear to be Anglo or "White," there is no ethnic representation among their students. Furthermore, the school community presents a rich source of ethnic heritage and multicultural backgrounds for the children to investigate. This activity draws on these possibilities in the school community and in the classroom as well. It stimulates the children as well as the teacher to discover "my ethnic neighborhood."

Objectives:
1. To provide opportunities for children to understand the heritage and ethnic groups represented in their own classroom, school and community.
2. To increase appreciation for the multicultural nature of the school community.
3. To stimulate activities that encourage children to explore the local community and the resources it offers.

Materials:

Copies of the questionnaire "My Ethnic Neighborhood" for each student.

Procedure:

1. Using a world map and a detailed U.S map, make the locations where the children's parents and grandparents lived before moving to their present community. In discussing the marks you have made on the two maps, ask the children such questions as: Do you think being from different areas and countries makes the people living in our community *now* different from each other? In what ways? Language? Foods? Clothes? Holidays and festivals?
2. Give each child a copy of the questionnaire "My Ethnic Neighborhood" to take home and have their family help them fill it out.

MY ETHNIC NEIGHBORHOOD

Purpose:

To explore and discover the different ethnic groups that exist in the neighborhood surrounding your school. Fill out the following questions to the best of your knowledge. Ask others in your neighborhood. You can use your phone directory to help you, too.

1. We have found that there are the following different ethnic or cultural groups in our community.

   _____   _____

   _____   _____

2. They sometimes speak a _____ language. And some of the words they use in this language are _____ , _____ , _____ _____ , _____ , _____ .

3. Some of the holidays celebrated are _____ , _____ , _____ .

4. Some of the favorite foods and dishes are _____ _____ , _____ , _____ , _____ .

5. Other items and artifacts, folk arts and crafts are _____ , _____ , _____ , _____ .

6. Our class (our school) can visit and talk with some members of this ethnic group at _____ during _____ .

7. Other questions and comments:

   My name _____

   My class _____   _____

   _____

Follow-up Activities:

1. When the children return the questionnaires, discuss their findings with them as a group.
2. Make a chart of the field trips and locations in the community that the children suggested the class visit.
3. Plan the community trips and write appropriate letters to prepare for the trips.
4. Finally, review and discuss what the children have found out about the ethnic composition of their school community. Consider preparing displays or programs for others in the school based on their findings.

WE ARE AN ETHNIC FAMILY

Introduction:

Role-playing is an excellent activity to help eight, nine, and ten-year-olds empathize with others. We know from child growth and development theories that children of this age are the most receptive to taking the role of the other and to projecting themselves into others' situations by fantasy and imagination. Making use of these qualities in the middle elementary school years is important to help children understand the feelings, attitudes and values of those who differ from them. This activity calls for role-playing the lifestyle and situation of an ethnic family.

Objectives:
1. To help children place themselves in the role of the other and to empathize with situations in life experienced from another viewpoint.
2. To provide oral language activities through dramatics and play-making experiences.
3. To motivate children to extend their range of literature and topics of interest in their reading.

Materials:

Obtain a filmstrip and cassette, film or video tape that presents the lives of children and their families from differing ethnic backgrounds. The Anti-Defamation League offers media materials of this type. If you cannot obtain media materials with this content, find several storybooks about the lives of ethnic families, such as:

Angelita, by Wendy Kesselman; Publisher: Farrar, Strause and Giroux or *In My Mother's House* by Ann Nolan Clark, Publisher: Viking Press.

Remember, whether you use filmstrips, films, books, or perhaps even a videotape the emphasis should be on the child and the family life that surrounds the child.

Procedure:

1. Discuss the various aspects of the family's existence as portrayed in the book or film. Talk about the role of the mother and the father, the children, or other relatives if they are present. Describe and analyze the setting, whether urban, suburban or rural.
2. After discussing the situations of the children and their families, have the students choose which ethnic families they would like to role-play. Divide your class into several conveniently sized groups of six to eight players. Have the children invent and practice their role-playing scenarios.
3. Give each group time to present the life of the various ethnic families to the total group. After each presentation, allow time to discuss the feelings and attitudes that arise in the role-playing dramas.

Follow-up Activities:

Invite the children's parents or grandparents of various cultural backgrounds to discuss their experiences in the family group with the children in your class.

USING MUSEUMS FOR ETHNIC EDUCATION

Introduction:

Do not overlook an outstanding—and usually free—source of inspiration and material for your program in ethnic education--the museum. Museums, both art and historical, are the repositories of America's ethnic heritage. Be sure to visit your local museums and obtain information about permanent and short-term exhibits. Talk with the curators and directors, tell them about your interest in ethnicity and the multicultural heritage of the geographic area and school community. They will likely respond with support for your plans.

Objectives:
1. To broaden and extend resources for ethnic education by using local resources—the museums in your area.
2. To familiarize children with museums, their resources and their personnel.
3. To provide added information and material for language arts, social studies and arts and crafts activities in your classroom.

Materials:

None required; resource materials are helpful.

Procedure:

1. Contact the director and curator of collections of your local art and/or historical museums. Find out about exhibits on various ethnic groups and heritages, either on display currently or planned for the future. Make arrangements for your class to visit the museum, or if feasible, have the museum official come to the school with displays. This is a good opportunity to involve parents and other adults in your classroom projects.
2. Prepare your class for the exhibits and ethnic heritages they will encounter at the museum. This can be done through geographical and historical sources, resource persons and audiovisual aids such as films, filmstrips, slides, and records.
3. Meet the school's visual requirements for field trips. Get parents' permissions. Schedule the outing.

Follow-up Activities:

Murals, artwork, chart stories, individual booklets by the students, thank-you notes to the visitors or to the museum personnel, replicas, displays and cultural arts programs are some of the wide range of activities that can follow ethnic heritage experiences generated by museum contacts.

THE MELTING POT VS. THE SALAD BOWL

Introduction:

The purpose of this activity is to help the students formulate their own feeling or meaning for ethnicity and its relationship to life in the United States. It is also designed to aid the students in understanding the terms acculturation and assimilation.

Objectives:
The teacher will demonstrate two experiments which can be made analogous to a melting pot society and multicultural society.

Time:

One class period.

Materials:

Five or six bottles of paint, the makings for a small salad: lettuce, slices of cucumber, slices of carrots, mushrooms, pieces of tomatoes, etc.

Procedure:

1. (The melting pot) In a clear glass, put about one-half inch of one color paint. Comment on the brightness and quality of color, and let the class view the paint. Name the color after an ethnic group (e.g., Irish Americans).
2. Put half an inch of another color of paint in the glass, being careful that it does not mix with the first color. Let the class name it for another ethnic group (e.g., Dutch Americans).
3. Tell the class that when groups of people come together and lose their old customs and traditions, they become assimilated. Mix the two colors of paint together until you can no longer identify the separate colors.
4. Continue adding the colors and naming them for ethnic groups and then mixing or making the assimilate into the whole.
5. After the process has been completed, ask the class to form a definition of the word assimilation and write it on the chalkboard.
6. (The salad bowl) In a glass bowl, tear up the lettuce and name it after an ethnic group.
7. Add each salad ingredient, naming it for a different ethnic group.
8. Mix all the salad ingredients together and then ask the class to identify the ingredients by the ethnic group's name.

9. Compare this to acculturation by telling the students that persons from different ethnic groups can live together and yet keep their identity by not losing their old customs and traditions.

10. Have the class form a definition of the term acculturation and write it on the chalkboard.

Follow-up Activities and Results:

One teacher remarked after trying this activity:

> Both analogies worked well, and I believe the children were able to give meaning to the terms assimilation and acculturation. This can be seen by the results of the post-tests asking them to define the two terms. It might be better to divide the lesson into two class periods on different days, because the lesson took more time than I expected.

MAPPING ROOTS

Introduction:
Children need to visualize the countries of origin of different class members. By providing a world map with strings showing these origins, the students are able to see that America is made up of persons from many countries.

Objectives:
All students who have found that their heritage has roots in other countries will place a string on the map from your state to their country of origin.

Time:
One class period.

Materials:
World map, string, pins, bulletin board.

Procedure:
Ask the students to come up to the bulletin board and pin one end of the string in your state and the other in their country of origin.

Follow-up Activities and Results:
The students enjoyed this activity, and it was helpful to those who thought Nebraska was another country.

The map bulletin board can become a center for attention. The children like to show their classmates their personal country or countries of origin. The display can also serve as a catalyst for discussions about ethnicity among groups of students on an informal basis.

SHARING THE DIFFERENCES—PART I

Introduction:

Children are interested in learning how to say things in a different language. If there are students in your class who are bilingual, then they can be used as resources. Otherwise, there are paperback dictionaries which can be used as a source for words and phrases of a different language. The object is not to learn a different language but rather to gain respect for other languages as valid means of communication.

Objectives:
Each student will make a small booklet in which he or she can put words or phrases from another language.

Time:

One class period.

Materials:

Construction paper, writing paper, stapler.

Procedure:

1. Have each student construct a booklet and design his or her own cover.
2. Let the students as a group decide what words or phrases they want to put in their booklets.
3. Write the words or phrases on the chalkboard so all students can copy them.
4. Tell the students that they can find out other words or phrases from other languages on their own if they desire.
5. In the days following ask students who have collected new words to share them with the class.

SHARING THE DIFFERENCES—PART II

Introduction:

Inviting, with sincerity, resource persons into your classroom can be an important contribution to multicultural education. It is beneficial to make the resource person and the children feel that it is an important event. Always reinforce the idea that a different culture's way of doing things is not "cute" or queer but rather "neat", different and valid.

Objectives:
Students will share in another individual's culture through listening and asking relevant questions.

Time:

One class period for each visitor.

Materials:

Any audio-visual aids which might be requested by the resource person.

Procedure:

1. Ask either a parent or another individual to be a resource person for your class. Explain the goals of your program and that you want students to be exposed to individuals with diverse backgrounds. Make sure the individual understands that your interests are genuine.

2. Ask the students to prepare questions ahead of time and put these on a chart. This is done to avoid having the entire period turn into "Will you say my name in your language?" It is also desirable for the children to have questions in mind so that they know what they want to learn from the experience.

Follow-up Activities:

One teacher remarked: The entire experience was delightful. Our resource person answered the children's questions with sincerity and it was a real learning experience. The children prepared the questions ahead of time, and there was much debate as to whether some of the questions should be asked. This was very good because it showed a true sensitivity on their parts.

The following is the children's list of questions:

1. How long have you lived in this country?
2. Did any American customs or traditions seem strange to you when you first came to this country?
3. What languages do you speak?

4. When relatives come, what language do you speak?

5. What does your writing look like?

6. Do you still write people from your homeland?

7. Does your family still practice any customs or traditions from your homeland?

8. How do the people in your country of origin dress?

9. Are there any fast-food places there?

10. Are your everyday routines the same here as they were where you were born?

11. Do you celebrate any special holidays?

12. How are children treated in the country where you were born?

13. Can you tell us about any special religions or beliefs that the people in the country where you were born have?

14. What types of homes do they have where you were born?

15. Do you fix any special foods that are different fom American foods?

16. Do you like living here?

A CREATIVE EXPERIENCE: DEVELOPING A MEDIA PRESENTATION

Introduction:

A culminating experience will give the children uses for what they have experienced and learned. A total class project involving creating a slide/tape show or a videotape offers just this type of opportunity. The class can feel very proud and the product serves as visible evidence of their learning.

Objectives:
Each child will select how he or she wishes to be photographed and in what type of setting. Each child will write a script telling about themselves and their ethnic heritage.

Time:

Varies on time required to take photos and tape scripts.

Materials:

Tape recorder, camera, film.

Procedure:

1. Tell the students that you want to make a slide presentation featuring them.
2. Ask each student to select where he or she would like their pictures taken.
3. Take the pictures.
4. Ask each student to write a script telling about themselves and their ethnic heritage. It is important to respect what each child says about themselves. Tell them to limit what they say to about a two-minute presentation.
5. Have the children read their scripts to you so you can help them if they cannot read their own writing or if it is not flowing. It is not necessary to change what they say, only to make it possible for them to read their scripts with ease.
6. Tape each other's script.
7. After the slides are developed, fit the slides in the order of the taped scripts, and the children's slide presentation is ready to be viewed.

Follow-up Activities:

The children were excited about making the slide presentation (or video tape). They were highly motivated to write their scripts. It took us about one week to get all the photos and the scripts taped. They were so proud of their work that they wanted to show it to the resource persons who visited the class, the principal, and other fourth graders in the school.

A TRIP TO A TOY STORE

Introduction:

When children are given a choice to pick their own toys at the store their selections could be influenced by certain assumptions about what is proper for boys or for girls to play with. Historically, toys have been imputed with gender-related attributes. Why has this occurred? What specific toys are associated with boys? with girls? How do toy manufacturers and advertisers, as well as toy stores use these traditional attitudes and values to sell their wares?

Objectives:
Students will gather information, sort and discuss their results to determine whether toy stores are influencing children in the purchase and use of toys by labeling them specifically for boys or for girls.

Time:

One day of classtime plus time outside of class—about a week.

Materials:

Checklist for a "toy search."

Procedure:

1. Pass out the "Toy Search" Checklist and discuss the directions.
2. Give the students time outside of the classroom to go to toy stores, hobby shops or sections of department stores where toys are sold, about a weekend or several days.
3. Have the students meet in small groups to share their findings by discussing: does the packaging influence decisions to purchase a toy? what specific skills and interests are important for using the toy? what made you think certain toys were just for girls or just for boys?

Follow-up Activities:

Ask the students to watch television commercials, especially on Saturday mornings, to see if toy advertisers are using gender stereotypes to present their products to children and their parents as consumers. Discuss what students and their families can do to change discriminatory practices.

Doing a Toy Search

Instructions: Make a trip to a toy store, hobby shop or the section of your department store where toys are sold.. Look over all the toys that are for sale carefully, notice the packaging. Are there some that indicate that the toy is only for girls? or only for boys? for either? Make a list using the headings as follows:

Name of Toy   Girls ONLY   Boys ONLY   EITHER Boy/Girl

Note: When you see that a toy has a certain indication on the package that the item is for boys or girls only, does this influence YOU? Compare your findings with other students in your class.

WHAT DO I CALL MYSELF?

Introduction:

This activity continues the exploration into self-concept and self-identity. However, it can be used to begin a discussion and study of ethnicity and pluralism, as well as allowing children to express themselves and identify the label or name they wish others to apply to them. Perhaps your students will reject the idea of giving themselves ethnic labels or religious labels like Catholic or Jewish. They may feel appropriate labels are ones like "human being," "boy," "girl," etc. Whatever the outcome, the discussion should prove provocative and stimulating, but be sure to make participation voluntary.

Objectives:
1. To introduce the children to the concept of their own identity.
2. To consider what labels (or absence of labels) the children apply to themselves.
3. To have children compare their own attitudes about labels with what others think of them.

Materials:

Copies of questionnaire "What Do I Call Myself?" for each student.

Procedure:

Instruct the students to number the labels on the student questionnaire "What Do I Call Myself" in the order that they feel applies to them. Explain that they are to put "1" next to the term that best describes them, the "2" next to the second most important term, and so on. Make sure they fill in the two questions at the end, as well. You might demonstrate by filling in the form for the class as an example. Give the students an opportunity to look over the labels and ask any questions or make remarks before they fill out the form.

Follow-up Activity:

Have the students discuss what responses they made to the questionnaire. This can be done in small groups or with the class as a whole. You can consider the following points:

1. Do all students in your class identify themselves the same way? How do you account for the difference in how individuals assign labels to themselves?
2. How many of your students label themselves **primarily** with an ethnic group or label? With a religious label? With identification by gender? Solely by their name?

One teacher found that her fifth-graders responded by identifying themselves as either a member of an ethnic group or as male or female. When she asked them the reasons for these identifying labels, they replied that one could be born a girl or boy, Chicano, Black, or White, and these were things that couldn't be changed. One child put it this way, "You are stuck with these labels every day so that they are important in your mind. If you don't like it, that's tough! But if you don't like your religion or other labels, you can change them."

What Do I Call Myself?

Instructions: (The teacher can read aloud these instructions to the children.) By yourself, number in order the following labels people might give you. Think carefully about what is most important for you to be called or recognized for. For example, if you feel it is most important to be identified as a "boy" or a "girl", place the number "1" in the space in front of that label. If you feel that no labels should be used for people at all, then place a "1" by the item "unique individual."

_____ Male

_____ Female

_____ Unique Individual

_____ Student

_____ Athlete

_____ Black

_____ White

_____ American

_____ African American

_____ Mexican American

_____ Native American

_____ Other group _____ (what?)

_____ My given name

_____ Human Being

1. First of all, I call myself _____

2. I think others call me _____

WHAT DO I CALL MYSELF?

On your own, rank order the following labels according to their importance in your life. For example, if you feel it's most important to identify yourself as a unique individual, place the number "1" in the space in front of that label. If you would identify yourself as a Teenager second, place a "2" in front of that lable. If you feel labels should not be important at all in your life, place a "1" by the item "prefer no label for myself," and do not bother to rank order the rest of the items.

_1_ American

___ Catholic

___ Protestant

_2_ Jewish

___ Other religious group? ___

___ Teenager

_3_ Male

___ Female

_6_ Student

___ Athlete

___ Black

_7_ White

___ Mexican American

___ Afro American

___ Chicano (a)

___ Hispano

___ Spanish American

___ Arab American

___ Irish American

___ Oriental

___ Native American

___ Other radical group? ___

___ Other ethnic group? ___

_9/8_ My given name

_4_ Human being

___ I prefer no label for myself

___ Labels other than those listed

_____

_5_ Unique individual — not like everybody else arond me, have some special qualities that noone else has.

Most importantly, I call myself __An American Jew(ish)__

_____

I think others would primarily label me

__American.__

_____

WHAT DO I CALL MYSELF?

On your own, rank order the following labels according to their importance in your life. For example, if you feel it's most important to identify yourself as a unique individual, place the number "1" in the space in front of that label. If you would identify yourself as a Teenager second, place a "2" in front of that lable. If you feel labels should not be important at all in your life, place a "1" by the item "prefer no label for myself," and do not bother to rank order the rest of the items.

_____ American

_____ Catholic

_____ Protestant

_____ Jewish

___1___ Other religious group? _penticostal_

_____ Teenager

_____ Male

_____ Female

_____ Student

_____ Athlete

_____ Black

_____ White

_____ Mexican American

_____ Afro American

_____ Chicano (a)

_____ Hispano

___2___ Spanish American

_____ Arab American

_____ Irish American

_____ Oriental

_____ Native American

_____ Other radical group? _____

_____ Other ethnic group? _____

_____ My given name

_____ Human being

_____ I prefer no label for myself

_____ Labels other than those listed

_____

_____ Unique individual

Most importantly, I call myself ___female_____

_____

I think others would primarily label me

___Chicana_____

_____

144

HOW IMPORTANT IS ETHNICITY TO ME?

Introduction:

This activity uses a questionnaire to help students think about the importance of ethnicity in their own lives and the lives of their families. You may find that some students, particularly those who are mainly Anglo-American or from a mixture of ethnic backgrounds, will show a lesser degree of ethnic identification than will students who identify with ethnic minority groups, such as Black, Mexican American, Puerto Rican and Asian American, or white ethnic groups of Southern European ties, such as Italian American and Greek American. This "start-up" activity should provide the foundation for further investigation in the area of ethnic studies in your curriculum.

Objectives:
1. To recognize the importance of ethnic identification and group consciousness in the student's personal family identity and heritage.
2. To provide a basis for investigating the concept of ethnicity and one's own ethnic identity.
3. To further skills in the language arts and provide content for the social studies that springs from the student's own sources for investigating the social world.

Materials:

Copies of "How Important Is Ethnicity to Me?" for each student.

Procedure:

1. It is worthwhile to provide some stimulation for the questionnaire before giving it to your students to take home and fill out. Here are some suggestions for pre-questionnaire activities.
   a. Hold a short discussion with your students, focusing on the key terms dealing with ethnicity. Ask them what they think it means to be an ethnic. What is ethnicity? An ethnic group? You will probably touch on terms like "customs," "immigrants," "ancestors," "another country or homeland" or "speaking a different language." Try to identify and clarify these ideas for your students before they answer the questionnaire. Review the definitions of terms in Chapter One before you hold this discussion.
   b. If it is possible to do so, locate a filmstrip, film or book that presents the concept of ethnicity.
   c. Bring in a resource person to whom the students can administer the questionnaire. Perhaps you, another teacher, your administrator or another adult in the school can serve as the resource person representing an ethnic group or the ethnic experiences in America. Have one of the children interivew the resource person as an

example of what each child will be doing when he or she completes the questionnaire. Then discuss how the person interviewed responded. What terms were used in some of the answers?

2. After you have prepared the students to use the questionnaire, distribute copies of "How Important Is Ethnicity to Me?" to all students. Instruct students to fill it out as a homework assignment. Explain that information from parents and relatives will probably be necessary in completing this questionnaire.

Follow-up Activities:

1. The next day or shortly after the questionnaires are filled out, hold a follow-up discussion of what the students discovered. If you have used some type of pre-questionnaire stimulation, refer to issues and questions raised in that group discussion. Be sure to ask the students about any problems or concerns they may have run into when filling out the questionnaire.

2. Ask how many students learned things about their ethnic identity that they hadn't realized before. Encourage students to comment on what they learned from filling out the questionnaire. If some discovered that their families came to America as immigrants, use this opportunity to enlarge upon the concept of immigration, perhaps initiating further activities that could center around this information.

3. For those students who have concluded that ethnicity means little to their own identities, stimulate a discussion of why this seems to be so. Some students may remark that they feel more American than Greek, Irish, or some other nationality or ethnic subgroup; encourage them to analyze the source of their feelings.

How Important Is Ethnicity to Me?

Purpose:

Are you an ethnic? How can you find out? Here are some questions that you can ask your parents, grand-parents and your relatives to help you find out how important your ethnic group is to you and your family.

1. Were you born in the United States? _____ Yes _____ No

2. Was one or neither of your parents born in the United States? _____ Yes _____ No

3. How many of your grandparents were born in the U.S.?

   0   1   2   3   4

4. How many of your great-grandparents were born in the U.S.?

   0   1   2   3   4   5   6   7   8

5. List the countries from which your ancestors came:

   _____ _____ _____

   _____ _____ _____

   _____

6. What language is spoken in your home (at least most of the time)? _____ English _____ Spanish

   Other _____

7. Has your family always spoken the same language? _____ Yes _____ No   If not, what other

   languages were spoken? _____

8. Has your family name been changed at any time in the past? _____ Yes _____ No   If so, when

   did it change? _____ Why was it changed? _____

9. Does your family keep ties with another country? _____ Yes _____ No   If so, in what ways does

   your family keep these ties? _____

10. Has your family changed the religion/church they attend or belong to? _____ Yes _____ No

    If so, when did these changes occur?

11. Do you or other members of your family have close relatives living in another country? _____ Yes

    _____ No   Do you keep in communication with these relatives? _____ Yes _____ No

12. Do you consider yourself to have strong ethnic identity? _____ Yes _____ No   Why or why not?

    _____

"OUR ETHNICITREE": A BULLETIN BOARD PROJECT

Introduction:

After the students have learned something of their family background by completing the "How Important Is Ethnicity To Me?" questionnaire, suggest they prepare a bulletin board in the classroom to depict the different heritages represented in the group. The bulletin board can be headed, "Our Ethnicitree."

Objectives:
1. To provide opportunities for students to develop a personal understanding of ethnicity.
2. To provide opportunities for students to appreciate diversity within their own classroom group.
3. To provide opportunities for language arts and social studies activities in a multi-ethnic context.

Materials:

Bulletin board, construction paper, tacks, photos, drawings, family tree charts, artifacts, etc.

Procedure:

1. Using the results of the questionnaire "How Important Is Ethnicity To Me?" or "My Ethnic Family Tree" chart found earlier in this book, have the children design a bulletin board display for the classroom.
2. Example of "Our Ethnicitree" bulletin board:
   a. Picture frames, display pictures of relatives or photos of locations of origin.
   b. Display shelf to exhibit ethnic artifacts or family heirlooms.
   c. Family tree charts with family names, pictures of photos if available.
   d. Remainder of bulletin board is decorated in colors, pictures, and items representing each child's heritage.
3. Plan for and discuss changing the Ethnicitree bulletin board periodically.

Follow-up Activities:

1. Hold a class discussion on the results of the Ethnicitree bulletin board. What new knowledge and understanding have been gained? Who noticed and reacted to the Ethnicitree bulletin board? Would other school personnel like to contribute to the Ethnicitree bulletin board?
2. Some variations or themes for the Ethnicitree bulletin board could be a feature on family customs, including dress, wedding and social conventions, travel and food habits or traditions.

RANKING YOUR FEELINGS

Introduction:

The purpose of this activity is to have students choose among alternatives and then examine what their responses reveal about their own ethnic and gender attitudes. Students are asked to number in order their feelings about issues which concern various ethnic groups in American society and the relationships among them. After the children have identified their preferences among competing alternatives, class discussion can emphasize that many issues related to ethnicity and gender require much more thought and consideration than they first realized. If you have already used the questionnaires presented "What Do I Call Myself" and "How Important Is Ethnicity to Me?" you can draw from these experiences, as well, in discussing issues of ethnicity and gender identity.

Objectives:
1. To examine children's attitudes toward various groups in our society.
2. To stimulate consideration of the relationships between groups, and to examine feelings about these ties or animosities.
3. To have a starting point for study and discussion about ethnicity, gender, and pluralism in American life.

Materials:

Copies of questionnaire, "Ranking Your Feelings," for each student.

Procedure:

1. The teacher should explain that this is a "forced-choice" activity, that some students may not like any of the choices presented, but that they must pick one anyway.
2. Instruct students to place a "1" by the item they most agree with a "2" by the item they next prefer.
3. After the students have filled out the questionnaire, organize discussion groups of three or four students each. Let the students talk about their choices and how they arrived at them. Have each group select a reporter who will present to the class as a whole the choices of his or her group.

Follow-up Activity:

When you have completed the activity, consider what issues and conflicts arose from the small group discussions. What further points of study do the results suggest to you.

Ranking Your Feelings

Directions: Place a "1" by the response you most agree with and a "2" by the response to the situation you next feel most comfortable with.

1. Which would you rather be?

   _____ African American

   _____ Mexican American

   _____ Irish American

   _____ Arabic American

2. In our school, what would you most like in relation to gender integration; that is, boys and girls in separate schools or the same school?

   _____ all schools are for both boys and girls

   _____ separate schools—i.e. girls only; boys only

   _____ combination of the two above with freedom to choose one's own type of school

3. Where would you least like to live?

   _____ in a ghetto in an urban city

   _____ in a barrio in an urban city

   _____ in a small rural village

   _____ on a mountain side, five miles from a town

4. What do you consider the most serious problem in our cities today?

   _____ discrimination in jobs and housing

   _____ transportation

   _____ hunger

   _____ homelessness

5. Which would you be most willing to do?

   _____ serve in the armed forces

   _____ serve in a civilian corps to help homeless and sick people

   _____ work in an urban ghetto

   _____ work on an Indian reservation

6. If you were a slave crossing the ocean on a slave ship, which would you most likely do?

   _____ revolt

   _____ jump overboard

   _____ refuse to eat

   _____ go along with the situation, be passive

7. If you went to your local supermarket and there were people outside passing out leaflets asking you not to shop there because of poor working conditions for the migrant lettuce pickers and grape growers, what would you do?

_____ shop there anyway

_____ go to another market for your food

_____ shop at the picketed supermarket but not buy any fruit

_____ join the picketers and help pass out leaflets

8. What would you do if you saw racial or ethnic conflict starting in your school in the lunchroom or the lavatory?

_____ go immediately to the principal's office and tell school officials about it

_____ stay as far away as you can get from the conflict

_____ try to break it up

_____ join the altercation

USING YOUR OWN SCHOOL AND CLASSROOM
FOR INTER-ETHNIC EXCHANGES

Introduction:

Sometimes we search far and wide to find "foreign" students or other "foreigners" to visit our classrooms and tell about the culture or ethnic group they represent. Despite our good intentions, we are prone to overlook possibilities that are right under our noses. This activity calls upon the teacher to examine the ethnic backgrounds and heritages of the class members and to promote exchanges and cross-cultural experiences right within the classroom and the school. The most successful exchanges are carried out with the direct involvement of the children's parents. In today's complex society, there are more parents who actively seek cross-cultural experiences for their children to help them learn to live in a multi-cultural society. Try to identify such parents in your school community and work with them in planning and carrying out these inter-ethnic exchanges.

Objectives:
1. To use the classroom as a laboratory for inter-ethnic experiences.
2. To help students realize that their own classmates offer opportunities for experiencing and understanding other ethnic groups and subcultures.
3. To discover, through classroom exchanges and contacts, the variety of ethnic groups within the local community.
4. To allow students to experience firsthand what it means to function in a different atmosphere or ethnic subculture with unfamiliar values, customs and folkways. Also, to impress upon children that cross-cultural experiences can take place close to home, in their own neighborhood and school.

Time:

One to two weeks.

Materials:

None.

Procedure:

1. Identify the ethnic backgrounds and heritages of the students in your classroom. Assess the possibilities for exchanges of living experiences between members of the class. Use discretion when suggesting and arranging inter-ethnic visits among students. Students who are hesitant to participate in the first or second try-out of this activity should have their preferences honored.

2. Begin the exchange experiences with students who volunteer (often these will be the ones with parental support for such an exchange) and those who seem mature enough to handle a day or two in a home which may be strange to them. You may want to begin by arranging inter-ethnic experiences among four or six students, paired to exchange home and family experiences over a weekend, two days or one night. Again, try to involve parents who express interest in such an activity. When these exchanges prove successful, you can move on to arranging longer visits.

3. Following the weekend exchange, have the students discuss their experiences with the class, allowing at least twenty minutes to half an hour for discussion and questions. Develop a list of items that the exchange students can think about and consider during their visits. Have the exchange students describe what they saw, ate, heard and did during the weekend in each others' homes.

Follow-up Activities:

1. Have the students who participated in the exchange experiences write a short paper or essay on what they felt and thought during their weekend in another ethnic group home. Did they gain any insights about their own identity and ethnic affiliations as a result of the experience.

2. Analyze the other students' reactions to their classmates' descriptions of the inter-ethnic experiences by (a) giving a short-answer questionnaire on the opinions of the experience, and (b) asking for volunteers for the next round of exchanges.

3. Develop a graph or chart on the ethnic groups represented in your classroom. Have the students prepare the chart and discuss the various heritages and traditions that are represented.

4. Attend festivals or other special occasions of the various ethnic groups represented on the chart and in the community. Or invite representatives of the ethnic groups to your classroom. See what cultural events—music, drama, dance, art—can be introduced into the curriculum to perpetuate the lessons of the inter-ethnic exchanges.

WITHIN MY OWN FOUR WALLS

Introduction:

To underscore how close tangible evidence of ethnic diversity can be to the student, suggest they begin by looking in their own homes for evidence of the contributions different groups have made to the habits and conveniences of our everyday lives. This famous quote from the anthropologist, Ralph Linton makes the point eloquently:

> Our solid American citizen awakens in a bed built on a pattern which originated in the Near East but which was modified in Northern Europe before it was transmitted to America. He throws back covers made from cotton, domesticated in India, or linen, domesticated in the Near East, or wool from sheep, also domesticated in the Near East, or silk, the use of which was discovered in China. All of these materials have been spun and woven by processes invented in the Near East. He slips into his moccasins, invented by the Indians of the Eastern woodlands, and goes to the bathroom, whose fixtures are a mixture of European and American inventions, both of recent date. He takes off his pajamas, a garment invented in India, and washes with soap invented by the ancient Gauls. He then shaves, a masochistic rite which seems to have derived from either Sumer or ancient Egypt. Returning to the bedroom, he removes his clothes from a chair of southern European type and proceeds to dress. He puts on garments whose form originally derived from the clothing of the nomads of the Asiatic steppes, puts on shoes made from skins tanned by a process invented in ancient Egypt and cut to a pattern derived from the classical civilizations of the Mediterranean, and ties around his neck a strip of bright colored clothe which is a vestigial survival of the shoulder shawls worn by the seventeenth-century Croatians. Before going out for breakfast, he glances through the window made of glass invented in Egypt, and if it is raining puts on overshoes made of rubber discovered by the Central Indians and takes an umbrella invented in Southeastern Asia. Upon his head he puts a hat made of felt, a material invented in the Asiatic steppes (Linton, 1936, 326–7)

A passage such as this really impresses on students that they need only look around their own homes, even their own bedrooms, to find evidence of the contributions many cultures have made to our daily lives.

Objectives:
1. To use daily experiences and objects at hand to highlight the multi-ethnic heritage of our society and the many ties we maintain to cultures and nationalities around the globe.
2. To share ideas about these taken-for-granted sources of our daily customs and the objects we use for these common practices.

Materials:

None.

Procedure:

1. The teacher can use the Linton statement or make some other introductory statement to highlight how many of our everyday objects and customs derive from the wide range of cultures and ethnic groups that make up American life.

2. Assign students to explore one room of their own homes—the kitchen, the living room, etc.—and make a list of the objects they can find that originated in another country or culture. Many objects have stamped right on them, Made in _____ , or others can be assessed by asking parents or grandparents or by consulting an encyclopedia, dictionary or other reference text.

3. Have the students bring their lists of objects to class the next day. They should also have collected some general information on the culture from which the objects originated. Choose various students to present their lists and discuss them.

Follow-up Activities:

1. If the students seem enthusiastic about this activity, have a contest to see who can come up with the most diverse and the longest list. Or, have the students compete in tracing the objects back to various heritages and ethnic groups, with points for elaboration and evidence of research.

2. Have students keep track of where they found the information for their lists. How wide a range of adults or sources gave them information? Did they use the local museums or historical societies?

3. Another way to classify common objects in one's house might be to identify those things that have their origins in the United States (like the moccasins in the Linton quotation) and those objects that originate in other countries and areas of the world, such as Europe, the Middle East, the Far East or South America. Have the class discuss various interesting categories.

A CHECKLIST ON ETHNIC AND GENDER EDUCATION
FOR YOUR SCHOOL

Introduction:

It can be meaningful for children to assess the extent and influence of ethnicity, gender, and multicultural perspectives in their own school. One technique for evaluating ethnic and gender influences in the school's policies and curriculum is to come up with a checklist for determining the school administration and community's attitudes toward these concerns in the school.

Every teacher should be deeply aware and sensitive to the social and political climate of the school and community. In some schools, a checklist assessing ethnic and gender influences will be readily received with eager responses. Unfortunately, in other school communities such an activity can be inflammatory and ill-received. Before engaging in the activity suggested here, ascertain the climate of your school and community. Discuss the checklist and its function with your principal and possibly with some of your children's parents as well. Be sure you have the support of your school staff for this undertaking. The results of your checklist will prove more significant if they are solicited in a receptive atmosphere.

Objectives:
1. To systematically collect data about attitudes and values regarding ethnic and gender education in your school
2. To analyze the importance of ethnicity in your school by evaluating the data collected.

Materials:

Copies of "A Checklist on Ethnic and Gender Education for Your School" for each student.

Procedure:

1. Make sufficient copies of the checklist for all students and teachers involved in the activity.

2. Discuss with your students a feasible plan for administering the questionnaire to individuals in the school. Include teachers, administrators and students in the sampling.

3. Assign the teacher, a group of students, or a neutral party to tabulate the responses gathered.

4. Provide a means of reporting the results of the poll to the total group, such as preparing a transparency or making a chart or master list of the results on the board.

5. Discuss with the class how they stand on each of the items in the guidelines, i.e., how many responded "strongly," "somewhat," "hardly at all," etc. to the various items on the checklist.

6. Hold a class discussion on the conclusions that can be drawn from the results of the questionnaire. Discuss how ethnicity and gender awareness is treated in your school.

Follow-up Activity:

Create a program to emphasize the needs for ethnic and nonsexist education in your school based on the findings from the checklist. Try to involve the principal, school administrators and parents in the school community.

A Checklist on Ethnic and Gender Education for Your School

You have been selected to participate in a school survey conducted by _____ class in the _____ School. Below is a list of statements. You are asked to place a check mark in one of the three columns by each statement. You do not have to answer all the statements. Your participation is voluntary. Should you decide to include other comments, please do so on the back of the survey.

Thank you for your time and consideration.

_____
                              Signed

Question	Rating		
	Many	**Some**	**Hardly**
Do you think there are different ethnic groups in your school?	————	————	————
Are different ethnic groups recognized in your school curriculum, books, materials, by the teachers and students?	————	————	————
Are different roles and opportunities for women recognized in your school curriculum, by teachers and students?	————	————	————
Do school assemblies, speakers, holidays, reflect the presence of different ethnic groups? and for girls and women?	————	————	————
Does your school library or resource center have a variety of materials on ethnic groups and women?	————	————	————
Do outside and after-school activities include most ethnic groups as well as boys and girls present in your school?	————	————	————

Question	Rating		
	Strongly	**Somewhat**	**Hardly at all**
Does the general school policy recognize the needs of different ethnic groups and different patterns of behavior?	————	————	————
Do school policies make provisions for recognizing and celebrating holidays and festivals of various ethnic groups in the school?	————	————	————
Does the school hold inservice training for teachers in multicultural and gender studies?	————	————	————

HOW IMPORTANT IS ETHNICITY TO ME: A RE-EXAMINATION

Introduction:

Once you are well into your program of ethnic and multicultural education, it is a good idea to re-evaluate the effect of the exercises and activities on the children. This can be achieved by asking them to complete the student handout, which is a follow-up to the "How Important is Ethnicity to Me?" activity present earlier in this book.

Objectives:
1. To evaluate your students' understanding of the meaning of ethnicity and ethnic group identity.
2. To determine if the students have changed their attitudes about the concept of ethnicity.

Materials:

Students handout of evaluation questions.

Procedure:

1. Present the students with the following handout of evaluation questions.
2. Compile the results of the questionnaire from your class and discuss the results with the group. Have the results provided new insights into your students? New insights and understandings about yourself and your school?

Evaluation Questions

Based on your present feelings about your ethnicity:

1. I am a person with a strong ethnic identity. _____ Agree _____ Disagree

2. The way I feel about my ethnicity has _____ has not _____ changed since we began studying about ethnic groups in our country.

   Comments _____

   _____

3. My family's ethnic ties are important to me. _____ Agree _____ Disagree

4. The emphasis on ethnic groups and on differences among peoples is dangerous. I feel we should try to forget our cultural and ethnic differences and recognize ourselves as Americans first _____ Agree

   _____ Disagree

5. As we have been studying about ethnic groups, I have become more aware of my own ethnicity and would like to find out more. _____ Agree _____ Disagree

6. The subject of ethnicity is NOT important to me at this time. _____ Agree _____ Disagree

7. The subject of gender awareness IS important to me at this time. _____ Agree _____ Disagree

Follow-up Activity:

Read the responses on this questionnaire with care. Hold appropriate discussions with your students in small groups or individually as fits the situation.

ACTIVITIES FOCUSED ON THE
ASPECTS OF ETHNICITY*

*As presented and discussed in Chapter One of this book.

THE REFUGEE EXPERIENCE

Introduction:

An activity such as roleplaying is particularly appropriate to help children understand the plight and experiences of the refugee forced to leave one's homeland against one's wishes. To stimulate interest and empathy for roleplaying the refugee experience, the teacher may want to obtain the outstanding and deeply moving file "Becoming American: The Odyssey of a Refugee Family", from New Day Films, P.O. Box 315, Franklin Lakes, New York 07407 Phone (201) 891–8240, 58 minutes, rental, $85.

Objectives:
  1. To help students empathize with the situation of the refugee.
  2. To encourage students to use roleplaying to understand the situations of others.

Time:

One to two class periods.

Materials:

Film suggested above or other stories, films or filmstrips about refugees. The text: Shaftel F., and Shaftel G. *Roleplaying in the Curriculum.* Prentice Hall, 1982.

Procedure:

  1. Have the students view the film suggested or discuss with students what it means to be a refugee. Point out that refugees are forced to leave their homeland, usually for political, religious or economic reasons, while immigrants are those people who choose to leave their country. Ask students to examine their feelings about leaving their home to go to a strange place. Would they know the language of the people where they have travelled, the customs, and traditions, the ways of obtaining food and services?
  2. Encourage several students to volunteer to plan a roleplay of the refugee situation. Suggest to the "actors" in the roleplay the following points:
     a. Is this a family leaving together for a new country or just some of the members of the family? What would they say to each other? How would they react to the leave-taking?
     b. What possessions would one choose to take along if one was never to return to the homeland again?
     c. Who will help the family to go to the new country? Who does the family expect will help when they arrive? Have the students discuss these various points to incorporate in the roleplaying situation.

3. Carry out the roleplay of becoming a refugee, or refugee family. Allow the "actors" to continue in the situation as long as it seems appropriate.
4. When the roleplay comes to a close discuss the feelings of the "actors." Encourage the "audience" of the other students to comment on the situation.

Follow-up Activities:

Suggest that another group of students develop the roleplaying situation of a refugee family. Try the roleplay again. What new or different interpretations have arisen? Discuss.

STEREOTYPING ETHNIC GROUPS AND GENDER ROLES
IN THE DAILY NEWSPAPER

Introduction:

Today we expect our daily newspaper to be sensitive to stereotyping of ethnic groups, particularly of ethnic minority groups such as Blacks and Hispanic people and of using gender-neutral terminology. But how carefully do the reporters and editors, as well as the general policy of the newspaper, adhere to the tenents of these practices? This activity encourages students to examine how free of ethnic and gender prejudice and stereotyping the local, daily newspapers actually are in their reporting of daily events and activities.

Objectives:
1. To encourage students to observe closely and become aware of stereotyping and prejudice in the local newspapers.
2. To help students better understand forms of covert racism, sexism and ethnocentric thinking.

Time:

One to two class periods.

Materials:

Several copies of the local daily newspaper.

Procedure:

1. Have students gather a number of copies of the local papers. Ask them to examine the papers for the following:
   a. Reporting of the news: Pick out the major news stories carried on the first pages of the paper, or sometimes on the back page. How many stories were about Anglo ethnic groups? How many stories were about non-Anglo ethnic groups? What were the activities of both Anglo ethnic group members and non-Anglo ethnic group members about? What caused the newspaper to report on the event or situation? How were descriptions of men and women handled?
   b. Newspaper photos: Examine the photographs that accompanied the articles. How many photos were of Anglo ethnic group people? How many of non-Anglo people? What were the people doing in the photos? Were the photos positive images, enhancing the reputation or career of the people, both men and women, involved, or negative images?
   c. Other sections of the newspaper: Examine other sections of the newspaper such as the advertisements for the movies, the homemakers section, the sports section. Are their ethnic and gender stereotypes reflecting in the reporting of this news? What

roles do the articles and pictures depict for the various ethnic/gender group members involved in these sections of the newspaper?

2. Have the students divide into small groups of four to five students and work on this project. Suggest the students develop a pictorial or graphic way of reporting their findings.

3. Bring the entire class back together when the project of examining the local paper is completed so that each group of students can share their results with the entire class.

Follow-up Activity:

Have the class present their findings to another group of students or interested parents or teachers.

HISTORICAL ASPECTS ACTIVITIES

REPOSITORIES OF ETHNIC HERITAGE: THE HISTORICAL MUSEUM

Introduction:

An outstanding and usually free source of inspiration and material for the program in ethnic education is the historical museum. Historical museums are the repositories of America's ethnic heritage. Be sure to visit your local historical museum and obtain information about permanent and short-term exhibits. Talk with the curators and directors, tell them about your interest in ethnicity and the multi-ethnic heritage of your school and school community. They will likely respond with support for your plans.

Objectives:
1. To broaden and extend the resources for the historical aspects of ethnicity.
2. To familiarize children with various types of museums, such as the historical museum.
3. To provide added information and material for other areas of the curriculum such as language arts, social sciences, art and music.

Time:

One to two class periods (or more).

Materials:

List of local historical museums and national museums that send out catalogues and other materials, i.e. The Smithsonian Institution in Washington D.C.

Procedure:

1. Contact the director or curator of collections of your local historical museum. Find out about exhibits on various ethnic groups and heritages, either on display currently or planned for the future. Make arrangements for your class to visit the museum, or if feasible, have the museum official come to the school with displays. This is a good opportunity to involve parents and other adults in your classroom project.
2. Prepare your class for the exhibits and ethnic heritages they will encounter at the museum. (Some museums are now featuring exhibits and shows of famous women in various fields, too.) This can be done through resource persons, and audio visual aides such as films, filmstrips, slides and records.
3. Schedule the museum visit and discuss what has been viewed when the class returns from the field trip.

Follow-up:

Murals, artwork, individual booklets by the students, as well as thank you letters to the museum personnel and building replicas of historical displays are some of the wide range of activities that can follow the visit to the historical museum.

WHAT WE CAN LEARN FROM HISTORY

Introduction:

Through roleplaying we can put ourselves in the place of others and empathize with their situation. Through roleplaying we can go back in time to historical events and attempt to feel firsthand what it was like to experience a particular historical happening. *In 1942* during World War II, President Franklin Roosevelt issued the Executive Order which authorized the internment of Japanese Americans who lived on the West Coast of the U.S. This activity suggests that students roleplay the situation.

Objectives:
1. To understand that discrimination and prejudice in the past during times of tension and stress such as a country at war, can produce injustice and unfair treatment toward various ethnic groups in the U.S.
2. To deepen historical knowledge and relate its implications to ethnic identity.

Time:

One class period.

Materials:

Shizuye Takahsima's *A Child in Prison Camp* N.Y. Tundra Books of Northern New York, 1971. A firsthand and forthright account of a girl's experience in a Japanese internment camp in Canada during the 1940s with drawings that illustrate the situation.

Procedure:

1. Discuss with the class the historical events surrounding the Japanese American internment camps during World War II and how they came into existence. Ask the students to react to how they would feel if they were forced to leave their homes and were placed in such camps.
2. Encourage students to volunteer to roleplay the situation. Carry out the roleplay and discuss. Use of the references suggested or other materials now available on the former Japanese-American Internment camps would provide information and facts for the students in presenting and discussing this roleplaying situation.

Follow-up Activity:

Suggest to students to research other examples in history where the U.S. or other countries designated specific ethnic groups as dangerous aliens and placed them in special camps, as well as restricting their rights or appropriating their land and possessions.

GEOGRAPHIC ASPECTS ACTIVITIES

WHO ARE THE IMMIGRANTS?

Introduction:

Previously we discussed the plight of refugees. Now we have discussed migration and immigrants in relation to geographic aspects of ethnicity. The concept of immigration is intimately tied to an understanding of ethnicity. Children at upper elementary school levels are beginning to empathize and identify with others, they can also grasp intellectually what it means to immigrants to begin their new lives in America.

Objectives:

1. To introduce children to the concept of immigration and its relationship to the concept of ethnicity.
2. To help children identify the immigrant heritage in their family backgrounds.
3. To provide an opportunity for students to discuss the meanings of prejudice, discrimination, acceptance and cultural pluralism with concrete examples.

Materials:

Films, filmstrips or records on the immigrant. Stories such as: "Levi Strauss, Forgotten Pioneer" in the text, *Many People, One Nation* edited by Peter I. Rose (Random House, 1972) or other appropriate stories.

Time:

One to two class periods.

Procedure:

1. Try to utilize your knowledge about the ethnic group membership of the students in your class or your own ethnic identity. Begin discussion with the class by asking, "What is an immigrant?" "Do you know any immigrants?"
2. Show the class some pictures of immigrants and the conditions under which they left their host or native land. Ask the question, "Why do you think these immigrants left?" Possible responses include:

    Because they did not like the climate.
    Because they didn't have a good water supply for crops and gardens; or there was a drought in their land.
    For better jobs.
    Because they were curious and wanted to see other places in the world.

They did not like the government of the country.

They wanted better living conditions.

Because a major disaster occurred such as a flood or earthquake.

3. Suggest the class develop a mural depicting the movement of the immigrants from their native land or country to America. The mural should show where in the U.S. the immigrants settle and what type of work or professions they choose.

Follow-up Activity:

Encourage small groups to further research the lives and careers of various immigrants with books such as: "Levi Strauss, Forgotten Pioneer" in the text listed above (the story of a successful immigrant), *Puerto Ricans: Island to Mainland* by A. H. Kurtis (N.Y.: Julian Messner, Simon and Shuster, 1969 (a book that includes photographic records of the immigration of Puerto Ricans to the U.S.), or *World of Our Fathers* by Irving Howe, Harcourt, 1975 (award winning compendium of the waves of Jewish immigrants that came from Eastern Europe to the U.S. in the 20th century).

TESTING YOUR GEOGRAPHIC I.Q.

Introduction:
Geographic facts about the countries of the world, in fact their very existence, are in constant flux and change. Especially in the past several decades since the close of World War II, students need to be informed about the changing geography of the world. Using books or atlases such as *The State of the World Atlas* by Michael Kidran and Ronald Segal (N.Y.: Simon an Shuster), this activity stimulates students to recognize the importance of the geographic aspect of ethnicity.

Objectives:
1. To encourage students to be aware of the importance of geography in understanding ethnic identity.
2. To motivate students to investigate the geographic influences upon people and their modes of living.

Materials:
The State of the World Atlas or other atlases and geographic materials.

Time:
One or more class periods.

Procedure:

1. Have students respond to the following questionnaire:

We often think we know more about the geography of the U.S. and the world than we really do. Many of our assumptions are based on misinformation. Respond to each item on the list of statements that follows by marking the blank (_____) by each item:

    Either   M—Misinformation
                    F—(Statement of) Fact
                    U—Undecided

Then discuss and compare your decisions on each item with other students in your class.

Questionnaire
  _(F)_ Africa is a continent of racial, cultural and geographic diversity. (Fact)

  _(F)_ India and Burma have been independent states since 1945.

  _(M)_ The U.S. and Western European nations are declining in population growth rate, while Mexico and Venezuela are increasing in their growth rates of population.

  _(F)_ Foreign workers have been arriving in increasing numbers to the U.S. in recent years.

__(M)__ Immigrants seeking work in Britain and Northern European nations have been growing in numbers during the late 1970s.

__(F)__ Foreign workers have been arriving in Saudi Arabia in growing numbers during the 1970s.

__(M)__ Many of the nations in South America are considered the rich nations of the world.

__(F)__ There are more telephones per 1,000 population in the U.S. and Switzerland than anywhere else in the world.

__(M)__ Argentina has a very low rate of literacy.
(sources of information; *State of the World Atlas*)

2. Now assign students to develop a questionnaire or list of their own containing various geographic, political and social facts about the U.S. and other nations.

Follow-up Activity:

Have students present their questionnaires to the class.

LINGUISTIC ASPECTS ACTIVITIES

OUR LANGUAGE: ENGLISH—HAS A FAMILY TREE

Introduction:

Many words in our English language are related to words in other languages because they all stem from one source: the Indo-European language family. Students will recognize the similarities when they can compare lists of familiar words such as "mother" or "father" in languages that are part of the Indo-European group of tongues. The teacher can help students to understand the relationships of language families by constructing a bulletin board depicting a "Language Tree."

Objectives:
1. The students will be able to see the relationship among different languages, their similarities and differences.
2. Students learn about the history of their own language background, a relation to other languages.

Time:

Three to four class periods.

Materials:

As listed in this activity.

Procedure:

1. The teacher should prepare a list of common words in several languages of Indo-European background. The students can get an idea of how English varies from other languages. The language of each student's cultural heritage should be included in this list. The students themselves can research a common list of vocabulary words by looking in foreign language dictionaries, asking parents or grandparents, other native speakers of the specific language field.
2. On a bulletin board, labeled "Language Tree," the students can make leaves for the various branches with the words they have researched.
3. Ask students to name languages that do not belong to the Indo-European language family. Names they may suggest include:

Chinese	(Sino-Tibetan)
Japanese	(Japanese and Korean)
Hebrew	(Hamito-Semitic)
Navajo	(American Indian)
Hungarian	(Ural-Altaic)

4. After the class has accumulated a list, have them look up the languages to find out which languages are related to each other. There are many language families besides the Indo-European and some include languages with many speakers.

Follow-up Activity:

Have students research how many people speak each language. They can prepare a chart of the most widely spoken languages in the world. Figures can be obtained by counting the population of countries that speak a particular language, or you can use information on what languages people learn as a second language. Check figures in almanacs and encyclopedia. Because the population of China is large, more people grow up speaking Chinese than any other language. However, English is the most widely used second language.

Examples of vocabulary words for mother and father:

	Mother	Father
English	Mother	Father
Irish	mathair	athair
Spanish	madre	padre
French	mere	pere
Italian	madre	padre
Portuguese	mae	pai
German	mutter	mater
Swedish	moder	fader
Russian	maty	otyets
Dutch	moeder	vader
Latin	mater	pater
Greek	meter	pater

ENGLISH BORROWING AND ENGLISH IN OTHER LANGUAGES

Introduction:

English is a mixture of many languages. Although English is historically related to German, it has been heavily influenced by French and has borrowed words from many other languages it has been in contact with. Words that were borrowed a long time ago are now considered part of English. Words borrowed recently usually show their foreign origins. When students look up word origins in the dictionary, point out that any word that does not come from Old English must have been borrowed and come into the English language at some time.

Objectives:
1. Students will learn the close relationship of language and culture through the use of common words.
2. Students will be aware of words which are cognates—those directly from another language.

Time:

One class period.

Materials:

As listed below.

Procedure:

Prepare a list of cognates, words other languages have borrowed from English and words English has borrowed from other languages. Have students prepare their own list of French or Spanish cognates or borrowed words they can find. Examples of words and cognates:

Language	Word	Cognates
Malay	ketchup	curiosidad
Arabic	alcohol	formalite
German	kindergarten, sauerkraut	associazione
French	souvenir, menu, encore	famoso
Hindi	shampoo	delicieux
Spanish	bonanza, mosquito	colore
Dutch	cole slaw, sleigh	bicicleta
American Indian	squash, raccoon	dictionnaire
Italian	macaroni, piano	dentista
Yiddish	kosher	aeroplano
Japanese	kimono	moderne
Scandinavian	smorgasbord	memoria

Follow-up Activity:

Have students exchange their lists of words and discuss as a total class.

ESPERANTO: THE UNIVERSAL LANGUAGE

Introduction:

The following paragraph is written Esperanto. It is an artificial language invented to be used as an international language. It is easy to learn and easy to understand because it is completely regular. Spanish-speaking students will find Esperanto much easier to understand than will English-speaking students because it is based on the Romance languages.

La inteligenta persono lernas la interlingvon Esperanto rapide kaj facile. Esperanto estas la moderna, kulture lingvo por la internacia mondo. Simpla, flekselbia, praktika solvo do la problemo do universala interkompreno. Esperanto meritas vian seriozan konsideron. Lernu la interlingvon Esperanto!

Objectives:
1. The students will understand and discuss the idea of a common world-wide language.

Time:

One class period.

Materials:

As stated in paragraph above.

Procedure:

Introduce the paragraph in Esperanto. After talking about the meaning, the students should discuss the possibility of a universal language and perhaps even a universal culture. Is it possible? Is it desirable?

RELIGIOUS ASPECTS ACTIVITIES

HOLIDAY GREETING CARDS

Introduction:

Ethnic groups celebrate holidays, festivals and special religious occasions whether they are recognized by the majority group of the society or not. Often the custom of exchanging holiday greeting cards is part of the celebration of the specific festival or occasion. Most holidays commemorating an important religious occasion like Christmas or Easter in the Christian faiths, include the custom of exchanging or sending out a greeting card with religious symbols, words or phrases of inspiration and holy significance to family and close friends.

Objectives:
1. To obtain and examine holiday greeting cards to determine the commonly held tradition of celebrating important religious holidays across diverse ethnic and religious groups.
2. To learn more about the holidays, celebrations and traditions of other religious and ethnic groups.

Time:

Two class periods (or more).

Materials:

Examples of ethnic greeting cards. These can be collected through parents, from greeting-card stores or other sources.

Procedure:

1. Discuss with students the background of religious freedom in the American tradition and the separation of church and state in the American public school. Use the information from this book's discussion on the religious aspects of ethnicity to help stimulate interest and awareness of religious diversity among American ethnic groups.
2. Ask students what manifestations of religious celebrations are evident in American society. Guide the discussion by focusing on the custom of exchanging holiday greeting cards during certain religious holidays such as Christmas and Easter in the Christian faiths and in mainstream or majority American culture generally.
3. Make an assignment to the students to collect examples of religious holiday greeting cards. What diverse holiday cards can they find or obtain from various sources? Suggest the student look for: Jewish New Year's greetings, Muslin holiday or festival cards (now available from UNICEF), Buddhist, Hindu or other religious greeting cards or calendars, posters with religious art and sayings.

4. After allowing a week or so for collecting these cards and other materials, have the students share with the total class their "finds." Discuss the symbols and the meanings in relation to religious holidays of the various ethnic groups represented. If the students do not know the meanings of the various sayings and symbols on the cards and posters, encourage them to research this information and report on it to the class at a later date.

Follow-up Activity:

Have students, either in small groups or individually, write papers and then put together a chart or album on what information they collected on the various holidays and festivals of differing religions, as a result of the religious holiday greeting card activity. Share this collection with others, as well.

SCHOOL VACATIONS FOR RELIGIOUS HOLIDAYS

Introduction:

Differing religious organizations and their churches, temples and mosques feel that students of the particular religious affiliation—Jewish, Muslim, Hindu, etc.—should be allowed a special holiday for religious occasions of their faiths. The argument is often that Christian students are given Christmas and Easter vacations as part of the regular school calendar, then why should not students of other religious affiliations have their religious holidays recognized in the school calendar? For example, Rosh Hashonah, the Jewish New Year: Id-al-Fitr, an important Islamic holiday; or Diwali, the Hindu Festival of Lights. This activity looks into the issues and problems which arise over this religious aspect of ethnicity.

Objectives:
1. To examine how the religious aspects of ethnicity become an issue for consideration in the everyday life at school.
2. To help students become aware of the diversity of religious affiliation and practices.
3. To emphasize the need for the recognition of ethnic pluralism and religious pluralism in America today.

Materials:

Use of the anecdote or similar situation as described below.

Time:

One to two class periods.

Procedure:

1. Present the following anecdote to the entire class: Before school starts two students, Betty Cohen and Mary White are talking.

   Betty: Tomorrow starts the Passover and I have to help my mom prepare for our seder, our special meal, so I won't be coming to the music program. Will you tell Mrs. Wright why I am not here?

   Mary: Oh yeah, I'll try not to forget. Boy, Betty, you Jewish people have really got it made! You had a vacation for *your* holiday in September at the Jewish New Year, and you got Christmas vacation off, too, so you get to take off on *our* holiday as well. And now you have another holiday this month.

   Betty: No reply, but just a pained expression on her face, responds with "uh-h-h?"
2. Have the students divide up into groups of 4, 5 or 6 students and discuss the issues and implication of this anecdote. What about other religious groups' holidays and occasions? What solutions could they suggest?

3. Bring the entire class together and have each small group share with the total class their ideas and points made in the small group discussions.

Follow-up Activity:

Have students write a short paper on this issue giving various alternatives for handling the variety of religious practices that effect school life, other than just the recognition of special holidays by taking a vacation from school.

SOCIO-ECONOMIC ASPECTS ACTIVITIES

IT'S OUR BUSINESS

Introduction:
Ethnic groups differ in the extent of private ownership of businesses within the community. In order to understand ethnic groups in the community students will develop a list of ethnic businesses and group by ethnic identification.

Objectives:
1. To develop an awareness of the variety of ethnic group ownership of private enterprise.
2. To develop an understanding of the importance of the goods and services provided by all private enterprise.
3. To utilize the telephone directory to locate ethnic private enterprise.

Time:
Two class periods.

Materials:
Telephone directories.

Procedure:
1. Divide students into groups of three to five and have one telephone directory per group.
2. As a total group, list as many types of private business as possible.
   Examples:
   1. Restaurants
   2. Shoe Repair
   3. Tailor
   4. Trash Collection
   5. Doctor
   6. Specialty Shop
3. Each group will make a chart with column heads of five different businesses. Each small group will research five different businesses. Next to each business students will list the ethnic group represented.
   1. Hispanic
   2. Italian
   3. German
   4. Native American

5. Polish
6. Vietnamese
7. East Indian
8. Blacks
9. English
10. Chinese
11. Cuban
12. Puerto Rican
13. Russian
14. Scandinavian

4. Students will list the business and ethnic group represented. The charts will be posted on the bulletin board.

Follow-up Activity:

Students will report back to the group regarding their findings. Students will then make a comparison of businesses most commonly occupied by various ethnic groups. Also find examples of people who are not engaged in stereotyped jobs, business and professions.

"SOCIAL CLASS LADDER"

Introduction:

Sociologists have noted that within a particular community, people can rank themselves and their neighbors according to power or prestige; that is they can assign different individuals to a particular position on a "social ladder." Individuals occupy positions within the various social classes based on various socio-economic aspects.

Objectives:
1. To view a community workers film and to place various individuals on a social class ladder.
2. To become aware of the social class distinctions within any community.

Time:

Three class periods (45 minutes).

Materials:

Films, videotapes, or filmstrips on community workers.

Procedure:

1. Show a community workers film or filmstrip and list all of the workers on the board.
2. Discuss the concept of social status as it relates to the various ethnic groups. Utilize this book as a guide to the discussion of social status.
3. List and discuss the five (5) social class divisions.
    1. "Upper-Class"
    2. "Upper-Middle Class"
    3. "Lower-Middle Class"
    4. "Upper-Working Class"
    5. "Lower-Working Class"
4. Ask students to rank the various community workers into the various classes. (Total class discussion)
5. Students are assigned a project to find 10 occupations and place them on a social ladder. (Students are given a ditto with a ladder and they can draw, cut pictures, or write the occupations on the correct rung of the social ladder.)
6. After the ladders are completed, have students share their ladders with the class. Discuss the various rungs as they apply to various ethnic groups. Do students feel that each ethnic group is equally represented on each rung?

Worksheet "Social Ladder"

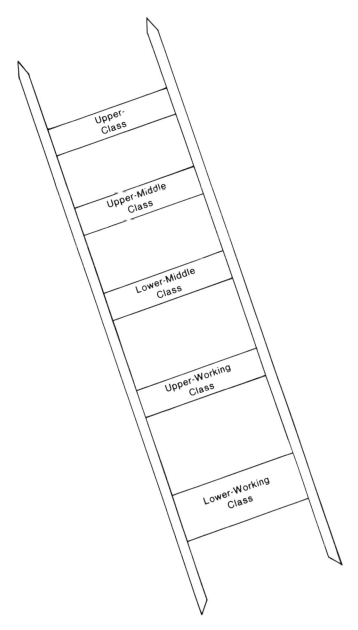

Upper-
Class

Upper-Middle
Class

Lower-Middle
Class

Upper-Working
Class

Lower-Working
Class

Follow-up Activity:

Have students utilize the U.S Department of Employment file or career books to research one occupation. They are to report back regarding the representation of the various ethnic groups. Students will share the results of their study with the class.

PRIVATE ENTERPRISE—AN AMERICAN DREAM?

Introduction:

Private enterprise requires an accumulation of wealth in order to finance a private venture. People with power have the necessary capital to finance a private business. This may restrict certain ethnic groups from participation.

Objectives:
1. To understand that private enterprise may be limited to certain ethnic groups.
2. To develop an awareness of the importance of the services provided by the various ethnic groups.

Time:

Two class periods.

Materials:

Strategies for Teaching Economics (Grades 4–6) by Marilyn Kourilsky, Joint Council on Economics.

Procedure:

1. Discuss private enterprise with the class discussing the concept of capital required to start a business.
2. Invite a speaker from the Small Business Loans office to speak regarding minority loans for business.
3. As a large group develop a questionnaire to use when interviewing an owner from an ethnic business. Also consider the aspect of gender, are some businesses difficult for women to enter?
4. Students will be divided into small groups (3–5) and participate in a field trip to various businesses to interview owners. (Parents would be contacted to serve as guides to accompany the students to the various businesses.) Prior to the field trip owners would be contacted for permission.
5. Students will report back to the group regarding their findings.

Follow-up Activity:

Students will write up a report about the owner they interviewed. Topics included would be as follows:

1. ethnic heritage and gender
2. type of business
3. difficulties encountered in starting the business

4. support from other agencies
5. support from family
6. success of business in the community
7. reason for opening business

POLITICAL ASPECTS ACTIVITIES

MINORITY HOLIDAYS

Introduction:

Holidays are primarily days set aside to celebrate religious, historical, or ethnic events. The holiday becomes nationally recognized whenever a political system designates it as such. Therefore, ethnic groups that are well represented politically are usually well represented with holidays.

Objectives:
1. To become aware of the various national holidays and the history behind each.
2. To develop an awareness of the ethnic-group representation and women represented in the legal holidays in the United States.

Time:

Two class periods (45 minutes each).

Materials:

Bulletin Board divided into six sections.

Procedure:

1. Make a list of all national holidays in which schools or businesses are closed, such as:
   1. Christmas
   2. Thanksgiving
   3. Labor Day
   4. Memorial Day
   5. President's Day
   6. Fourth of July
   7. Martin Luther King Holiday (in some states)
2. Divide students into six groups to research each holiday. The groups should find the reason for the holiday, who backed the thrust for the holiday, and what ethnic or other groups (women's/religious groups) are represented in each holiday.
3. Divide a bulletin board into sections. Have students visually present their research on the holiday.
4. Discuss the background of each holiday and the ethnic/religious/women's groups represented.

Follow-up Activity:

Students will propose a holiday for a selected ethnic group. Divide students into groups and have them choose an ethnic group to support. Once the group has a designated minority group to back, they must select a member of the group who has made a significant contribution to the broader society. Research the individual and his/her contribution. Propose a holiday and support your proposal with a rationale.

WHO GETS ELECTED IN OUR COMMUNITY?

Introduction:

Elected officials are backed by various groups; political, ethnic, and social. The elected official is generally the one with the greatest power group backing. Utilize the information in this book to discuss the political aspects as related to ethnicity.

Objectives:
  1. To understand how ethnic groups effect political elections.
  2. To develop an awareness of the difficulties faced by women and ethnically diverse individuals in the pursuit of a political office.

Time:

Two or more class periods.

Materials:

If available, advertisements, flyers and ballots from local elections.

Procedure:

1. Review the basics regarding the election procedure in the community. (The fifth grade curriculum generally includes a study of elections.)
2. Students are to research the community political officials for the number of women or ethnic members.
    1. mayor
    2. city council
    3. representative from our district
    4. school board members
3. Students are to develop a questionnaire to use for interviewing women or ethnic group political officials. Include questions such as:
    1. What is your ethnic heritage.
    2. What ethnic, political or social groups supported your election campaign?
    3. Do you feel your election was affected by your ethnic or gender background?
    4. Do you believe ethnic/women's groups are well represented in political offices?
4. Students will divide into small groups (3–5) and select one woman or individual from a specific ethnic group to interview. A visit or phone interview will be conducted.
5. Students will report back to the group the results of the interview.

Follow-up Activity:

Students will make a list of state officials and their ethnic/gender group affiliation. A pamphlet will be prepared listing state offices, elected officials name, and ethnic group affiliation and gender.

MORAL ASPECTS ACTIVITIES

THE SCHOOL DRESS CODE COMMITTEE

Introduction:

A student's appearance and dress while attending school can become a major issue involving not only the individual, but the entire class and the school. This activity utilizes roleplaying the situation of a boy who comes to participate in school life bizarrely dressed (for American society) in the robes of his native country.

Objectives:

1. To develop situations where students can identify the dynamics of prejudice and stereotypical thinking.
2. To help students recognize the strengths of diversity and the positive aspects of uniqueness and individuality.
3. To create a roleplaying situation to stimulate empathy and understanding of others.

Time:

One class period.

Materials:

The roleplaying situation described below.

Procedure:

1. Present to the entire class the following anecdote or roleplaying situation:

   You are appointed to a student committee to monitor the dress code of the school. There have been numerous complaints from parents, teachers and students that some students have been arriving at school lately, sloppily dressed in dirty and torn clothing, in bizarre outfits, with strange hairdos (punk style) and so on. The student chairman of the committee with the designated teacher in charge, both state that sloppy and bizarre dress or oufits in this school cannot be tolerated any longer.

   But one student speaks out and states: "Look at Mohammed, he wears those long white robes with white pants and a special embroidered cap everyday to school. He says that is all the clothes he has and it was the right clothes for school in his country before he came to America. What do we say to Mohammed? His way of dressing is important to him. Do we tell him now he can't wear his kind of clothes anymore?"

   What would you do if you were a member of the students dress code committee? How would you handle Mohammed's situation?

2. Encourage volunteers from the class to roleplay the situation of the dress code committee. Allow the roleplay to continue to its appropriate conclusions. Discuss the results and suggested resolutions of the situation.

Follow-up Activity:

Revise the roleplaying situation with someone taking the role of Mohammed. Have Mohammed describe his feelings and reactions to the dress codes committee's rules and regulations.

A CLOSING CAVEAT: THE USE OF NON-SEXIST LANGUAGE

It is important to close this section on activities for encouraging the recognition of ethnicity and gender in the classroom of elementary schools in the United States, with a statement about language—written and spoken. We all know that as we speak so do we think, and as we think so do we speak (and write). Therefore, the words that come out of our mouths, reflect the ways in which we think; our opinions, attitudes and values. This makes the use of non-sexist and stereotype-free language in our oral and written communications essential if we are to prepare children to live as adults in a pluralistic and global society.

As Tetreault has so succinctly put it:

> We are presently in a period of challenging the male dominance over curricular content and over the substance of knowledge itself. Evidence of that challenge is our new understanding of the extent to which the curriculum we learned excluded (or included) women's traditions, history, culture, values, visions and perspectives. More difficult yet to ascertain is the impression that viewing human experience primarily from a male perspective with the authority of the school behind it has made on us. We are beginning to envision a curriculum that includes content about women and gender, one that interweaves issues of gender, with ethnicity, race, and class. (Tetreault, 1989, p. 124)

Educators, both men and women, need to realize that historically the authority for the construction and the codification of knowledge in Western, patriarchal society was male. A male bias affected the choice of definitions that our dictionaries sanctioned and institutionalized. Our language, written and spoken, is a system of meanings encoded largely by men—mainly Anglo men of middle and upper class status. Today in this country and elsewhere in the world, we are instituting major changes to bring a fuller equality and greater opportunities to individuals through the development of guidelines for nonsexist and non-discriminatory usage of language. These guidelines are being developed by publishers, business and professional associations, and teachers. It is incumbent upon teachers and educators, above all, to seek to demonstrate the crucial nature and the value of avoiding biased language in their teaching and in their everyday life.

12 A

AN ANNOTATED BIBLIOGRAPHY FOR THE TEACHER

This annotated bibliography for teachers includes books, journals and teachers' materials discussed in this volume, as well as additional items that support teaching in a pluralistic, multicultural, non-sexist, and globally-aware atmosphere. Some entries in this bibliography are classic contributions to the field, while others are the most current editions of books in multicultural, multiethnic, gender and global awareness for elementary school teachers and administrators.

Allport, Gordon, *The Nature of Prejudice,* New Jersey: Doubleday, Anchor Books, 1954.

This classic study details the dynamics and psychological mechanisms of prejudice and discrimination.

Banks, James. *Teaching Strategies for Ethnic Studies.* 4th Edition. Newton, Mass: Allyn and Bacon, 1987.

The author, who is noted for pioneering the field of ethnic education, has set forth goals, concepts and instructional strategies and techniques for incorporating the teaching ethnicity in elementary and secondary schools. This Fourth Ediction of one of the most outstanding and comprehensive texts on multiethnic and multicultural education available for teachers, includes even more references, ideas and materials than previous editions.

Banks, James. *Multiethnic Education: Theory and Practice.* Second Edition. Newton, Mass.: Allyn and Bacon, 1988.

In the Second Edition of a text designed to help preservice and inservice teachers clarify issues related to pluralistic and multiethnic education, Banks describes actions that educators can take to implement programs and practices for ethnic and cultural diversity in schools.

Banks, James and Banks, Cherry A. McGee. (Editors) *Multicultural Education: Issues and Perspectives.* Newton, Mass: Allyn and Bacon, 1989.

This collection of contributions on aspects of culture, ethnicity, social class, religion, gender, and exceptionality in education and teaching presents experts' views on these educational issues. The authors in this volume, astutely brought together by the Banks, call for substantial reforms in schools to provide every student with opportunities for equality in education.

Banks, James and Lynch, James. (Editors) *Multicultural Education in Western Societies.* London: Cassell, 1987.

This volume features chapters from educators in various nations who discuss multicultural education in crosscultural and international perspectives. It is an innovative attempt at comparative views on multiethnic and multicultural education in developed nations, and offers helpful insights to American educators on these worldwide concerns in education.

Bennett, Christine. *Comprehensive Multicultural Education*. Newton, Mass. Allyn and Bacon, 1988 Second Edition.

The author's desire is to provide both theory and practical applications for teaching multicultural education in our pluralistic society.

Boulding, Elise. *Building a Global Civic Culture: Education for an Interdependent World*. New York: Teachers College Press, 1988.

A well-written and far-reaching book that offers teachers new ways to view education for an emerging worldwide, civic culture.

Brown, Daphne. *Mother Tongue to English: the Young Child in the Multicultural School*. London: Cambridge University Press, 1979.

The goals of this book are to make teachers of young children aware of the special needs of those who come from ethnic minority groups and to give positive and practical help in meeting these needs.

Colangel, N., Foxley, C. and Dustin, D. *Multicultural Nonsexist Education: A Human Relations Approach*. Dubuque, Iowa: Kendall/Hunt Publishing Co., 1979.

A unique collection of readings that brings together the strands of human relations training, multicultural education and non-sexist education, this volume is an excellent resource book for teachers who wish to infuse their teaching with multicultural, non-sexist perspectives.

Fishman, Joshua. *Bilingual Education: An International Sociological Perspective*. Mass: Newbury House Pub., 1976.

Becoming a classic in the field, this book provides an outstanding synthesis of issues in multicultural education with an international, global viewpoint. The author, Professor Joshua Fishman, is one of the world's foremost sociolinguists. His prose is as elegant as the crucial message he brings about pluralistic education in global society.

Garcia, Ricardo, *Teaching in a Pluralistic Society: Concepts, Models, Strategies*. Second Edition. New York: Harper and Row, 1990.

Focusing on the crucial role of language in multicultural and pluralistic classrooms, Garcia provides teachers with his expertise and practicality in teaching in multicultural schools and teaching to prepare students to live in a multilingual world society.

Gilliland, H. and Reyhner. J. *Teaching the Native American*. Dubuque, Iowa: Kendall/ Hunt Publishing Co., 1988.

One of the few volumes available currently on specific teaching techniques and strategies for use with Native American students. The authors have incorporated the writings and teaching of Native Americans, but the information presented applies to teaching ethnically diverse children everywhere.

Gollnick, Donna and Chinn, Philip. *Multicultural Education in a Pluralistic Society.* Second Edition. Columbus: Merrill Publishing Co., 1986.

The authors discuss various microcultures to which they envision students belong. These are the microcultures of socioeconomic status, ethnicity, religion, language, sex and gender, exceptionality and age. In concluding, the authors bring together the rationale for the use of these insights in the teaching of pluralistic education.

Goodman, Maryellen. *Race Awareness in Young Children.* New York: Collier Publishing Co., 1964.

This is a classic volume in the field of race relations and multiethnic education. Though this book was researched and written over 25 years ago, it gives us insight and understanding of how racial attitudes begin among children by four years of age.

Hernandez, Hilda. *Multicultural Education: A Teacher's Guide to Content and Process.* Columbus: Merrill Publishing Co., 1989.

A thorough and carefully referenced text on teaching multicultural education at both elementary and secondary levels. The author includes in her text many resources and ideas for teachers of normal as well as exceptional children from mainstream and minority cultures.

Kohn, R.; Lutholtz, C. H.; and Kelly, D. *My Country 'Tis of Me; Helping Children Discover Citizenship Through Cultural Heritage.* Jefferson, Nor. Carolina: McFarland and Co., 1988.

A book of activities for young children that help build the concepts of citizenship through family membership, local community identity and finally, a national commitment.

Lynch, James. *Prejudice Reduction and the Schools.* London: Cassell, 1987.

The author gives counsel to teachers and educators on how to deal with racism, sexism, and general discrimination and prejudice in schools and in the broader society. This text focuses on classroom practice, the curriculum, whole school atmosphere and staff development when viewing prejudice and stereotyping.

Klein, Gillian with Bridgett Hill and Simon Wilby (illustrators). *Scrapbooks;* and *The Fancy Dress Party,* with Teacher's Guides. London: Methuen Children's Books, 1984.

Two series of five booklets each which feature the same children representing multiethnic heritages—Spain, India, West Indian, Hong Kong and Turkey. The storybook children's activities and experiences reflect those of children in early childhood classrooms everywhere.

Milner, David. *Children and Race Ten Years on.* London: Ward Lock, 1983.

The second edition of this classic research on prejudice and discrimination in childhood thinking, highlights studies of young children's attitudes and self-concepts of race in both the United States and England.

Noddings, Nel. *Caring: A Feminine Approach to Ethnic and Moral Education.* Berkley: University of California Press, 1985.

The nurturing and care-giver aspects of female socialization in most societies are the basis for the author's contentions that education needs these components in order to offer students a meaningful education for our modern world.

Ogbu, John. *Minority Education and Caste: The American System in Cross-Cultural Perspective.* New York: Academic Press, 1978.

A seminal research and discussion of the dynamics of minority ethnic affiliation in the United States and its impact on learning and equal educational opportunity. This book has been influential in focusing educators' concerns on teaching children of minority and majority groups in this country.

Ramirez, M. and Castaneda. *Cultural Democracy, Bicognitive Development and Education.* New York: Academic Books, 1974.

Another pivotal research study and findings that point to differences in learning styles based in ethnic minority membership and family heritage. These authors develop the thesis that learning is culturally conditioned and that teachers must be cognizant of these facts.

Sadker, Myra and Sadker, David. *Sex Equity Handbook for Schools.* New York: Longman and Co., 1982.

An outstanding resource book for teachers on all aspects of gender-neutral and non-sexist practices in education.

Sleeter, Christine and Grant, C. *Making Choices for Multicultural Education: Five Approaches to Race, Class and Gender and Turning on Learning.* Columbus: Merrill Publishing Co., 1988 and 1989.

These are companion volumes that set forth the authors' theories detailing five different approaches to teaching about race and ethnicity, gender, social class and exceptionality in schools and classrooms. The first volume provides teachers with a way of thinking about race, language, culture, class, gender and disability in teaching. The second volume offers teachers, at both elementary and secondary levels, exciting ways to infuse their teaching with their newly acquired awareness of these elements.

Journals and Newsletters

Educational Materials and Services Center. *Multicultural Leader.* Edmonds, Washington, 98020. Address: 144 Railroad Ave., Suite 107. Phone: (206) 775 3582.

This publication offers educators information about new publications, research studies, research reports and articles by leading authorities in multicultural, non-sexist and crosscultural education, both nationally and internationally.

Immaculate Heart College Center. *Global Pages.* Los Angeles, CA: 90064—Address: 10951 West Pico Boulevard, Suite 2021. Phone: (213) 470 2293.

Each issue features activities and projects for teachers that combine ethnic studies, gender issues and global perspectives for both elementary and secondary school levels.

Trentham Books, England. *Multicultural Teaching: To Combat Racism in School and Community.* Address: 151 Etruria Road, Stoke-on-Trent, Stafforshire ST1 5 NS.

Though published in England, this journal carries articles and book reviews, reviews of research and discussions of teaching projects and activities in multicultural, multilingual, multiracial classrooms around the world.

Index

Sadker, Davis, 17
Sadker, Myra, 17
Schwartz, Pepper, 42, 44
SCRAPBOOKS, 79–81
    Teresa's Scrapbook, 79–81
schools, 63
second language acquisition, 75–77
self-concepts, 34, 37–39, 89–90
sexism, 12, 85–88
    defined, 12–13, 14
Shakeshaft Carol, 12, 17
Sleeter, Christine, 84, 88, 97
social class, 9
    and aspects of ethnicity, 9–11
    and status, 9–11
social inequality, 22, 23
social studies, 51, 58
socialization, 41–42
    defined, 39
    and gender, 39
    primary, 39, 41–42
    secondary, 39
sociosphere, 91
Sprung, Barbara, 30, 32
Spatig, Linda, 42
stereotypes, 26, 35

students, 63
    exchange projects, 63–65
    expectations, 65
subculture(s), 38

teacher expectations, 30–31, 46
testing, 71–72, 78–79
Tetreault, Mary Kay, 198
textbooks, 86

University Park School, 49–51, 52, 53, 54
U.S. Census Bureau, 56

values, 4–6, 7–8, 9, 20

West, Susan, 50, 53
Western Interstate Consortium on Higher Education
    (WICHE), 70
Wilby, Simon, 79, 82
Wolfe, Tom, 41
women, 12–13, 14, 43, 85 88, 93
    girls, 12–13, 38–39, 42, 85–88
Wright, Jr. Roosevelt, 32, 44
Woods, Peter, 82

Index of Activities by Themes